Evolving Roles of
Sovereign Wealth Managers
After the Financial Crisis

Past, Present and Future

Evolving Roles of
Sovereign Wealth Managers
After the Financial Crisis
Past, Present and Future

Bernard Lee

HedgeSPA Pte. Ltd., Singapore &
Santa Clara University, California, USA

World Scientific

NEW JERSEY • LONDON • SINGAPORE • BEIJING • SHANGHAI • HONG KONG • TAIPEI • CHENNAI

Published by

World Scientific Publishing Co. Pte. Ltd.

5 Toh Tuck Link, Singapore 596224

USA office: 27 Warren Street, Suite 401-402, Hackensack, NJ 07601

UK office: 57 Shelton Street, Covent Garden, London WC2H 9HE

British Library Cataloguing-in-Publication Data

A catalogue record for this book is available from the British Library.

EVOLVING ROLES OF SOVEREIGN WEALTH MANAGERS AFTER THE FINANCIAL CRISIS
Past, Present and Future

ISBN 978-981-4452-47-2

In-house Editor: Yvonne Tan

For Melissa,
iamque opus exegi

Preface

In recent years, discussions related to sovereign wealth management are often framed under the ideological banner of "state capitalism".

Since the time of ancient Egypt, there is nothing novel about a state using its political and military clout to grow its national economic wealth. In more recent history, the Dutch East India Company and then the British East India Company did exactly that.

Under Adam Smith's enterprise model, the wealth of a nation is accumulated through the wealth of individuals. The state justifies its intervention when private enterprises cannot achieve economic objectives on their own. Such thinking led to the First Opium War.

Back in those days, the state did not directly own its private enterprises. Under the colonial economic model, private enterprises operated on foreign soils, but they were primarily owned and run by private citizens under colonial administrations, which *raisons d'être* were to maintain "law and order" for private enterprises to thrive.

After the Second World War, it was generally agreed that empires could only lead to atrocious conflicts one way or another. The state responded to voters' opinions and changed the way by which it manifested its role; nonetheless, the role of the state as the chaperon of national economic wealth was not diminished.

The military-industrial complex emerged in the United States and Western Europe in the 1950's. During the 60's and 70's, "state-assisted" capitalism resulted in the rise of the Japanese *keiretsu* business groups and the South Korean *chaebols*.

Until then, the state advanced its economic agenda primarily by helping private enterprises achieve their business goals. Typically, these private enterprises were run and majority-owned by its own nationals despite operating on a global scale.

What was changed in the 80's that led to the rise of the sovereign wealth management model, in which a nation's wealth was shifted toward investments in primarily foreign companies that were mostly run and majority-owned by foreign nationals?

One key story of sovereign wealth management began in a city-state in Southeast Asia known as Singapore[1]. A legacy of the British East India Company, this small island-state lacked natural resources and relentlessly reinvented itself to ensure its survival.

As Singapore gained its independence from the British, its young administration needed to find a practical solution to run a few newly-privatized enterprises including its telephone company, which was held by its Ministry of Finance at the time.

It moved these companies into a separate portfolio for more efficient management. As the city-state's economy and therefore its foreign currency reserves continued to grow, its central bank repeated the same successful formula and moved some of its staff into a separate entity to seek more interesting returns than those typical of foreign government bonds.

What happened in Singapore could be called a historical accident. Given its relatively small population of about 2.5 million in the early 80's, Singapore could not deploy its surplus wealth in a way that would emulate the success of the British East India Company. Faced with a growing foreign currency reserve clearly in excess of what would be required to defend its own currency, the only practical alternative to earning sub-optimal foreign government bond yields was to invest in foreign equities directly.

Not surprisingly, this formula of success was eagerly replicated by other countries, from the Norwegians to the Middle Eastern oil exporters, and then by the Chinese today. However, few rigorous studies have been conducted to fully understand the implications of this important yet subtle sea change in the global financial landscape.

Modern financial theories are driven heavily by borrowing the methods of the physical sciences. It is customary to assume that financial markets have infinite

---

[1]There is a non-conclusive debate as to whether Temasek Holdings or the Abu Dhabi Investment Authority should be considered the world's first sovereign wealth fund. Temasek Holdings was incorporated in 1974, while the Abu Dhabi Investment Authority (ADIA) was created in 1976. However, in 1967 Abu Dhabi created the predecessor of ADIA, the Financial Investments Board, which operated within its Department of Finance and was responsible for managing the Emirate's excess oil revenues. On the other hand, prior to the incorporation of Temasek Holdings, the Singapore Government had been managing its stakes on local companies via its Ministry of Finance since Singapore declared independence from Britain in 1963.

liquidity and are therefore friction-less, when the size of market participants is assumed to be small relative to overall size of the market.

Unlike the laws of classical mechanics, the very act of market participation can modify market outcomes. With mega-sized participants such as state investors, the net effects of such "distortions" to established financial models quickly add up.

This book aims to examine issues related to sovereign wealth management in the context of the following three questions:

(1) *Past Realities* — How did we get here?
(2) *Evolving Roles* — Do we understand what is happening today?
(3) *Future Directions* — Where should we go from here?

It is important not to underestimate the significance of this relatively recent development. Never before in history have countries invested such large portions of national wealth in financial (instead of physical) assets issued by other countries, which can be subject to defaults and bankruptcies.

According to testimonies given to a subcommittee of the United States Congress, an electromagnetic pulse device detonating over the American continent can knock out a significant portion of its power grid, thereby paralyzing a modern infrastructure that runs primarily on electricity. Throughout history, the major problems faced by human societies tend to be caused by a few weak links that are either taken for granted or conveniently ignored.

The financial crisis of 2008 showed that the same was true for the global economy. Let's think about a few hypothetical financial scenarios, as follows:

(1) If a major debtor country refuses to honor its debts, leading to a significant debasement of its currency, will that trigger a global economic meltdown among even the surplus countries, now that their foreign currency reserves and sovereign wealth funds may be worth significantly less than before?

(2) If the sovereign wealth fund of every surplus country rushes to invest in commodities, will the net result be a form of mass hoarding, which may drive up the prices of food and fuel, and leave impoverished millions in hunger and starvation?

(3) If the sovereign wealth managers of surplus countries simply aim to achieve market returns (commonly known as "beta") instead of firm-specific returns (commonly known as "alpha"), a standard investment thesis given the size of their respect investments, will that steer the world's surplus capital toward established firms, in effect driving capital away from innovative and potentially more productive ventures?

This book will not have answers to all these important questions. However, we will make an attempt to start a reasonable debate, which will hopefully give us satisfactory answers to these questions in time to come.

Bernard Lee, PhD, CFA
October 2013
Santa Clara, California, USA

Acknowledgments

The author would like to thank the Asian Development Bank Institute as well as the Institute of Southeast Asian Studies for sponsoring a manuscript, from which Chapter 2 of this publication has extracted relevant materials. Its research data was paid for by the China Investment Corporation. Special thanks are due to the Sovereign Wealth Fund Institute for providing a "refresh" on that data. The author would also like to thank Udaibir S. Das (International Monetary Fund), Hefei "Faye" Wang (University of Illinois at Chicago) and Ke Wang (Federal Reserve Board) for their kind and insightful comments on Chapter 3. In addition, the author wants to thank the participants of the Session on Sovereign Wealth Funds at the 2012 Annual Meeting of the American Economic Association held in Chicago for their comments and discussions on the materials presented in Chapter 3.

This book would not be possible without the author's earlier publications in *Sovereign Wealth Management* (published by Central Banking Publications and co-sponsored by the World Bank Treasury) and *Proceedings of the Joint BIS/ECB/World Bank Conference on Strategic Asset Allocation for Central Banks and Sovereign Wealth Managers* (published by Macmillan and sponsored by the European Central Bank). The author was invited to participate in such high-profile projects due to his prior employer BlackRock, to which he wants to thank once again.

Last but not least, the author wants to thank his many journalist friends in the media for constantly engaging him in public discussions on this topic. Theories and ideas can create useful social impacts only when the relevant individuals care to listen. With these valuable opportunities to take part in such discussions, the author is able to better understand the issues involved, and hopefully find a simple but effective way to communicate a complex subject matter to his audience.

Contents

List of Figures

List of Tables

Chapter 1

Overview

1.1 Are SWFs Potential Causes for Concern?

To put the activities of SWFs in context, total assets in the world at the end of 2010 summed to about US$198 trillion according to the McKinsey Global Institute[1]. Credit Suisse Research Institute assessed global wealth to be about US$231 trillion in mid-2011[2], while the International Monetary Fund (IMF) estimated the global holdings of equities, bonds and bank assets to be US$256 trillion[3]. Of course, a significant portion of global wealth can be classified as fixed assets that cannot be easily liquidated or reliably valued, such as primary residences, farmlands, jewelries and fine art pieces. Under the practical limitation of more precise valuations, aggregated global wealth was approximated to be about US$200+ trillion in 2011.

According to TheCityUK, in 2011 global SWFs were holding US$4.8 trillion in assets, with another US$7.2 trillion held by other sovereign investment vehicles and US$8.1 trillion held by foreign exchange reserves, or a total of US$20.1 trillion in assets being controlled by official institutions[4]. Capgemini and RBC Wealth Management estimated the investable net worth of High Networth Individuals (HNWIs) to be approximately US$42.0 trillion in 2011[5]. TheCityUK

---

[1] Charles Roxburgh, Susan Lund, John Piotrowski, *Mapping Global Capital Markets 2011*, McKinsey Global Institute, August 2011.

[2] Anthony Shorrocks, Jim Davies, Rodrigo Lluberas, *2011 Global Wealth Report Databook*, Credit Suisse Research Institute, October 2011.

[3] *Global Financial Stability Report, Statistical Appendix*, International Monetary Fund, October 2012, Table 1, Page 11. Estimate is based on the sum of global stock market capitalization, debt securities, and bank assets sourced from World Federation of Exchanges, Bank for International Settlements (BIS), IMF, International Financial Statistics (IFS) and World Economic Outlook databases as of 17 September, 2012.

[4] *Sovereign Wealth Funds*, TheCityUK, February 2012.

[5] *World Wealth Report 2012*, Capgemini and RBC Wealth Management, June 2012.

further estimated global pension assets to be about US$30.9 trillion in 2011[6]. Although not perfectly synchronized, the estimates above aggregate to US$93 trillion. Other liquid financial assets such as household cash and cash equivalents can be captured by global money supply index M2. Global 2011 M2 figures reported by the IMF summed to no less than US$40 trillion[7], part of which would be held by HNWIs and was therefore subject to some degree of double counting. However, generally speaking HNWIs tend to hold minimal liquid financial assets relative to their total assets, while non-HNWIs tend to hold limited liquid financial assets after excluding fixed assets such as primary residences. Roughly, estimates on the total global liquid wealth can be approximated to be about US$100+ trillion in 2011.

In other words, in 2011 approximately half of global wealth consisted of liquid financial assets, out of which roughly one fifth to one sixth was controlled by sovereigns and other official institutions. Is such a holding significant enough to create any potential cause for concern?

First of all, if one examines the balance sheet of global wealth, real estate is the single largest asset class. Not surprisingly, the bursting of any real estate asset bubble can lead to the collapse of all other related asset markets. That was roughly what we saw during the global financial crisis of 2008 and other earlier financial crises. It is unlikely that there will be any permanent and effective way to eradicate any such boom-and-bust cycles, as long as assets are priced based on free markets. The more practical question is whether there are counter-cyclical polices that can reflate asset markets without sowing the seeds of the next asset bubble.

From the balance sheet of global wealth, another potential contributor of instability is a major pension crisis, in which future liabilities grossly exceed funded assets. Such a phenomenon is already happening in a number of developed countries with aging populations that are facing reversed population pyramids. The solutions are well known — either the pension schemes must cut back on entitlement benefits, or there needs to be policy changes in areas such as foreign immigration that can restructure demographics effectively.

---

[6]*Pension Markets 2012*, TheCityUK, March 2012.

[7]M2 represents money and quasi money, which is comprised of the sum of currencies outside banks, demand deposits other than those of the central government, and the time, savings, and foreign currency deposits of resident sectors other than the central government. This definition corresponds to lines 34 and 35 in the International Monetary Fund's (IMF) International Financial Statistics (IFS). The problem with such a definition is that M2 is reported in local currencies country by country based on inevitably different accounting standards. Therefore, consistent aggregation becomes almost infeasible. The rough estimate provided is acceptable given the context it is used. As a quick sanity check, US M2 as published by the Federal Reserve was US$9.6 trillion at the end of 2011, and the US economy respresents roughly one quarter of nominal global GDP.

asset price by a large amount. As a result, a rational SWF asset allocator needs to price in once-in-a-decade "black swan" events ahead of making any allocation decisions.

To better understand SWF investing, we would like to expand on an idea pioneered by Nobel Laureate Robert Merton [Merton (1998)] for endowment investing, which describes how long-term wealth managers should consider the potential substitution effects due to anticipated inflow and outflow characteristics. Considering that global markets are dominated by three groups of countries with different national balance sheet profiles (as shown in Figure 1.1), it can be demonstrated how these countries will follow the following asset allocation policies:

(1) *Resource-rich countries (e.g. Middle Eastern crude oil producers)* — They are naturally "long" resources and "long" the global trade settlement currency (as a result of selling their natural resources). Their appropriate diversification policy is to sell resources forward and invest its global trade settlement currency reserves by buying manufacturing goods and intangible assets.

(2) *Exporting economies (e.g. East Asian export economies)* — As manufacturing powerhouses, they are naturally "short" resources and "long" the global trade settlement currency (as a result of producing and selling their manufacturing goods). Their appropriate diversification policy is to buy resources as well as intangible assets.

(3) *Deficit economies (e.g. the US and certain southern European countries)* — Their primary "exports" are intangible assets, such as equity and debt papers. Their appropriate diversification policy is to develop more value-added services (and hence intangible assets) related to resources and manufacturing.

In the absence of practical market constraints due to very large investments, any optimal asset allocation computed from such a model will recommend roughly the same optimum for all countries. The only expected difference is for a crude oil producer that is already "long" crude oil on its national balance sheet to accept an allocation recommendation net of its unextracted known reserves of crude oil.

To customize Merton's investment model for SWF investing, we need to go beyond stand-alone asset allocation models computed from the perspective of a single investor. Constraints at the global level matter for very large investors such as SWFs. The most obvious example is that there is only a finite amount of crude oil available globally, even after counting unextracted known reserves. The world may simply run out of any investable form of oil reserves, if all countries make simultaneous and significant allocations to crude oil. After imposing such hard

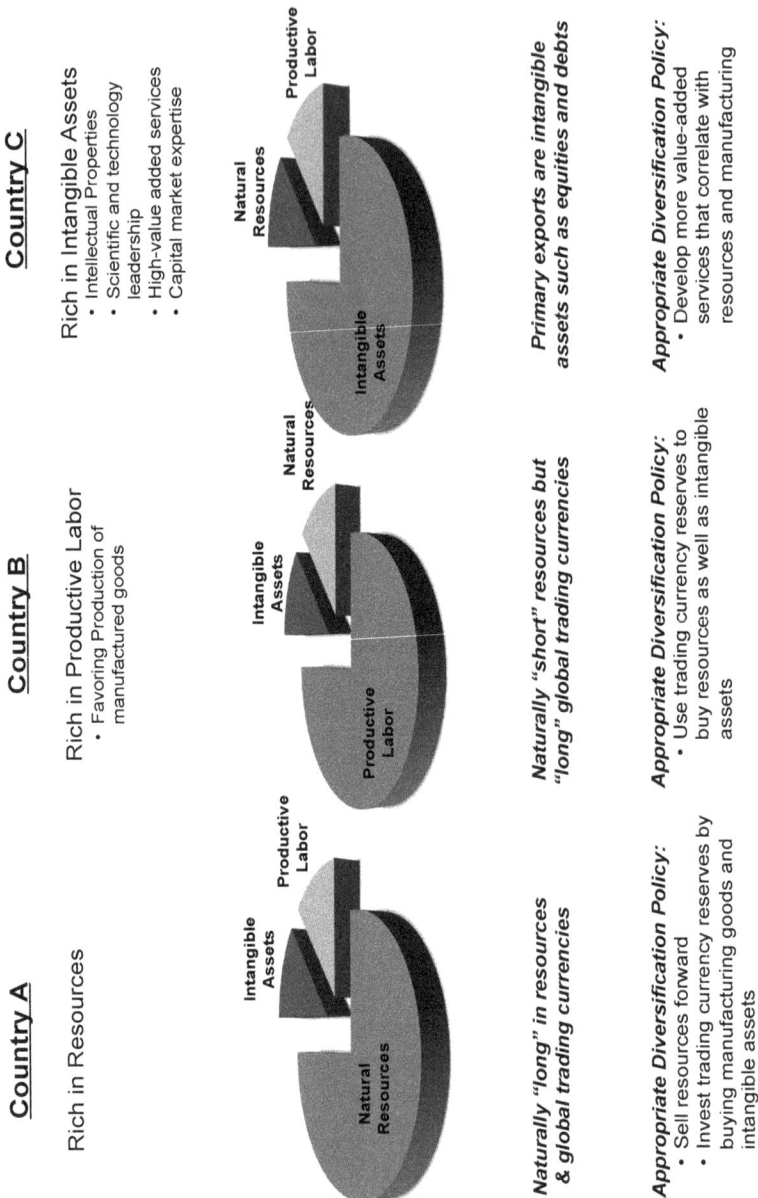

Country A

Rich in Resources

Naturally "long" in resources & global trading currencies

Appropriate Diversification Policy:
- Sell resources forward
- Invest trading currency reserves by buying manufacturing goods and intangible assets

Country B

Rich in Productive Labor
- Favoring Production of manufactured goods

Naturally "short" resources but "long" global trading currencies

Appropriate Diversification Policy:
- Use trading currency reserves to buy resources as well as intangible assets

Country C

Rich in Intangible Assets
- Intellectual Properties
  - Scientific and technology leadership
- High-value added services
- Capital market expertise

Primary exports are intangible assets such as equities and debts

Appropriate Diversification Policy:
- Develop more value-added services that correlate with resources and manufacturing

Fig. 1.1   Model of Global Economy in Lee (2006)

constraints, we may end up with infeasible solutions regardless of any brilliant mathematical formulations used.

Any asset allocation model that is meaningful to mega-sized investors such as SWFs must incorporate the plausible flows and aggregated constraints on the global economy into its mathematical formulation. Numerical results have shown that imposing such constraints at the global level may impact the final solution far more than the use of any sophisticated investment objective functions.

1.3 Implications to Global Imbalances

Based on the modified Merton's model as described in the last section, deficit countries need to issue debts and equities in order to finance imports and consumptions. Absent of any structural changes in the global economy, their wealth can be drained over time to pay for excessive imports and overconsumption. Tangible wealth will be gradually transferred from the deficit countries to the two surplus country groups. The accumulation of massive public wealth by the two surplus country groups is a logical outcome from such a model.

If the deficit countries consistently import excessively and/or overconsume, this global economic system can be sustained only if the economic values created by the deficit countries will be sufficient to pay for their imports and borrowing. In other words, the deficit countries can pay for imports either by borrowing or by making highly successful investments. There is nothing inherently wrong with such an approach, as long as the deficit countries can demonstrate consistent and exceptional investment skills.

However, there will be times when:

(1) the deficit countries run up so much debts that the rest of the world loses confidence that they can realistically create sufficient economic values to ever repay their debts;
(2) the deficit countries raise new debts primarily to roll over existing debts and to pay for consumptions; or
(3) there is a gradual shifting of high-value-added expertise in innovation and investment to the two surplus country groups, so the deficit countries may have a difficult time issuing equities and debts *ad infinitum*.

From that point in time, this global economic structure will become unsustainable.

It should be noted that the resource-rich countries can enjoy more purchasing power initially because of their relative abundance. The exporting economies will experience asset inflation over time, while the deficit countries will suffer from deflationary pressure, due to the gradual downsizing of its net assets. This is consistent with real-world observations.

1.4   Should there be Structural Solutions prior to Launching Rescue Attempts?

Are there credible structural solutions to persistent global imbalances? Must the world require any "rescue party" in shining armor in order to get out of the economic mess that it is finding itself in? Or, is it possible that some form of structural solutions would be the prerequisite to launching any rescue efforts?

To recap from the previous section, in order to avoid reaching any state of bankruptcy eventually, the deficit countries must do one or both of the following:

(1) Issue additional debts, so as to increase the amount of cash in hand; or
(2) Make successful investments, so that any increase in the valuation and/or dividend yield in equity holdings will be sufficient to fund their "burn rates" on national wealth.

The first solution (commonly known as "printing money", along with other more clinical descriptions, such as quantitative easing) has its natural limits. The surplus countries are unlikely to buy bonds issued by the deficit countries indefinitely, once they realize they will only be repaid in significantly devalued currencies (in terms of purchasing power), or when the deficit countries' debt loads become clearly unsustainable, defined as a level of debts being perceived by the financial markets as having insufficient incoming cashflows to service existing debts.

Therefore, the reliable driver to the deficit countries' medium-term economic process should be option 2. However, option 1 can be used to:

(1) "smooth" potentially volatile valuations and dividend yield payout patterns;
(2) better match the deficit economy's income-liability profile; or
(3) provide leverage on equity. After all, option 1 still matters because cash is king during highly unstable markets.

Assuming our description so far gives a reasonable description of today's global economy, are there potential structural solutions to "correct" global imbalances?

1.4.1   *Restoration of Gold Standard*

Restoring some form of Gold Standard roughly means that the issuer of the trade settlement currency makes a policy decision to fix its currency to certain units of commodities (usually gold or some other precious metals) on a specific date. From that point on, any new debts issued by the deficit countries will be effectively repaid in commodities, and there will be no practical difference between issuing debts and selling the underlying commodities forward.

Now the surplus countries have no investment rationale to buy such debts instead of the underlying commodities, without the deficit economies pledging their commodity reserves or another form of hard collateral, leaving the deficit economies without any effective mechanism to borrow simply by "printing" more money. With these structural constraints on issuing debts, it will be more logical for the deficit economies to raise funds by issuing as much equity that can be supported by the valuation and revenues linked to any new issuance.

Since equity value will then be measured against a rigid monetary base tied to commodity reserves, any increase in equity value will be traced back to actual increase in earnings or productivity. Thus, the mandate of managing public surpluses for the surplus countries become simpler. In any rigidly structured financial markets, there are fewer opportunities for those professional investment managers to profit by placing "macro bets" (beta investing, or betting on the relative values of key asset classes). Their investment managers will need to focus on picking companies that can create economic values (alpha investing via stock selection).

If the crisis is created partly by the deficit countries being too aggressive with "printing" money, such a crisis may deteriorate into a crisis of market confidence, once the deficit countries can no longer demonstrate that they are able to service debts already issued. Thus, instilling the discipline of a stable monetary base before the situation gets out of hand may help restore some degree of market confidence.

However, fixing the size of the monetary base will also make it challenging for the deficit countries to raise any additional funds that may be critical to the day-to-day functioning of its economy. This is a blunt solution in which one possible undesirable outcome may be the total collapse of the deficit countries' financial system and therefore economic activities, since they may have no other way to pay for key imports, such as fuel, on which restoring their economic health may depend.

1.4.2 *"Printing Money"* Ad Infinitum

This strategy will result in various global price indices increasing significantly over time.

The deficit countries' equity values will drop as discount rates of dividends increase (to compensate for the rapid loss of purchasing power by cash). Eventually, commodities with finite supplies will be the most likely asset class to hold its value. As in any out-of-control scenario such as hyperinflation, the logical response is for the surplus countries to hoard their commodities and/or delay any exports, so that the goods can fetch as high a price as possible under a rapidly devaluing currency.

Under this scenario, the only natural hedge available to protect the values of their overall investment holdings is for the surplus countries to allocate to commodities. The net effect may be a simultaneous allocation to commodities by investors, also known as mass hoarding. Mass hoarding can result in distortions in the efficient allocation of economic resources, since commodity prices will eventually reach a level that hinders productive economic activities.

Therefore, it is not obvious how this policy would necessarily help the deficit economy or the global economy restore their health.

1.4.3 *Issuing an Alternative Trading Currency*

Instead of simply letting the deficit countries print money *ad infinitum*, the surplus countries can act together to put an end to what is effectively a form of monetary union with the deficit countries.

If the deficit countries continue to issue more debts, the new debts will be primarily absorbed by the deficit economies' expanding monetary base. So the net result for the deficit economies may be severe inflation and rapid devaluation of their old trade settlement currency (relative to the new common currency). The deficit countries will therefore be disincentivized to run up unsustainable levels of debts in such a scenario, although it still has some ability to "print money".

The deficit economies will eventually lose its ability to import under the pressure of a depreciating currency and its exports are expected to become stronger, thus reducing any imbalance of payments within this global economic system over time. Barring any extreme scenario in which the deficit economies will reach bankruptcy before the necessary adjustments can be made, it is now feasible for certain structural adjustments to take effects, so that the global economy stands a chance to return to some form of equilibrium.

This solution is potentially more helpful than simply leaving the deficit countries under the structural constraints of a rigid global Gold Standard, which provides an extremely limited policy toolkit to restore balanced economic growth.

It is in the interest of surplus countries to help restore the deficit economies to health; otherwise, their investments (still priced in the old trade settlement currency) may rapidly depreciate in value. After the surplus economies have exited a *de facto* monetary union with the deficit economies, the risk for them to purchase any significant amount of the deficit countries' debts and equity are:

(1) inducing a runaway currency depreciation and domestic asset inflation in the deficit economies without necessarily restoring their economic health; and
(2) the surplus countries will be exchanging their new common currency for a potentially depreciating currency, resulting in some form of global economic contagion.

It should be noted that any new monetary union should be accompanied by responsible policies on forming fiscal and banking unions, so issuing an alternative trading currency will not provide any overnight remedy.

In summary, a structural solution by adjusting the relative prices of goods and services appears to be a pre-condition to reverse on-going and persistent imbalances. Only after the deficit economies find an effective solution to correct their habits to overspend, the managers of public surpluses can begin to deal with the legacy of past imbalances more effectively and invest in the deficit countries' economic recovery.

1.5 Can Sovereign Wealth Funds Save the Global Economy?

Let's now examine what SWF investment managers should do assuming that an acceptable structural solution can be identified and implemented.

1.5.1 *SWF Performance Objectives*

Like all investment managers, SWFs must first understand their performance objectives. By analyzing the drivers of a SWF's investment performance, we are able to analyze mathematically the conventional wisdom that allocating to an appreciating asset (relative to cash) is almost always positive regardless of investment horizons.

Because of their massive size, SWFs can "buy up" specific market segments, which is likely to be accompanied by a move in the opposite direction when they must eventually "cash out". That also means that it is only effective for SWFs to make long-term macro bets based on price changes reflecting fundamental changes in relative market values as a result of economic value creation instead of trading activities in financial markets.

A SWF should not be penalized for making a long-term investment, as long as such an investment can beat cash returns at the time of its exit. As a result, SWFs are in the position to pick companies, industry sectors or market segments that create long-term values (that complement its national balance sheet in the ideal case) or reflect fundamental changes in market values (commonly known as "alpha investing").

Their ability to hold onto their investments for much longer horizons than typical pensions and endowments (given the lack of any explicit liabilities) can provide them with significant advantages in any competition for capital.

In contrast, passive indexing (commonly known as "beta investing") often does not necessarily incentivize economic value creation, and may not automatically help SWFs realize their investment goals of complementing national balance sheets over a longer-term horizon.

Specifically, because net import/export is part of the national balance sheet, SWFs should be incentivized to pick not just valued-added investments, but also companies and sectors that complement existing profiles of national outputs.

1.5.2   *Intervening in a Financial Crisis*

We analyze two cases to determine whether it may be appropriate for SWFs to intervene in a financial crisis:

Case 1:

In order for SWFs to step in during a financial crisis, they are likely to lock in some investment losses by selling assets in a falling market, so as to fund any rescue attempt. Intervention will be appropriate when the SWF portfolio manager expects that its investments will under-perform cash and do so by significant amounts. The decision to raise cash under such circumstances suggests that:

(1) it is better to "unload" risky assets and invest in cash instruments if the expectation is that market will further collapse; and
(2) without a rescue, the rest of its investments may suffer so badly that on balance it is still in the best interest of a SWF to participate in a rescue effort, in order to support valuations in the rest of its portfolio.

Similar arguments were used to launch the rescues of certain global banks by syndicates of SWFs.

Case 2:

If the deficit countries' ability to generate cash is still a long way from meeting outflows purely from say debt servicing costs, then the situation may deteriorate into a solvency crisis. SWFs should demand debt restructuring before making further investments in the deficit countries' debts. This is similar to arguments used by some SWFs for their reluctance or refusal to participate in the capital infusion of certain European financial stabilization schemes.

The reality is that there may be no hard and fast rule for any SWF to distinguish Case 1 from Case 2, just like no central bank has identified a clear signal to distinguish a liquidity situation from a solvency crisis.

More often than not, a liquidity situation may simply deteriorate into a solvency crisis in a self-fulfilling prophecy, when countries in distress face further attacks from speculators. Once borrowing costs rise dramatically, the deficit country will no longer be able to roll over its existing debts and pay its bills. At the same time, the economic collapse of the deficit country may eventually hurt the surplus countries.

There is a mathematical condition under which intervention may be desirable. SWFs are likely to suffer initially as a result of participating in a rescue: They need to sell investments in a rapid declining market in order to fund any rescue attempt. If the rescue in a market crisis is successful, SWFs can benefit from "sell high, buy low". Once the rescue effort has turned the situation around, SWFs can deploy its cash and reallocate to investments at the now-market lows.

Realistically, one should expect that SWFs will still suffer because not all investments will come out intact in most financial crises. So failed investments will still impact the balance sheets of SWFs.

For exporting countries, as long as their net exports can still break even or become even slightly positive after all is said and done, a SWF has done its job in stabilizing the markets. From a self-interest viewpoint, an exporting country rarely wants to force deficit countries into any disorderly defaults, because exports may not recover after a disorderly default, and there is no guarantee that the values of its investments will hold up after deficit countries go into default *en masse*.

In contrast, a resource-rich country can afford to be less concerned because it is endowed with commodities, as long as commodity demands are sufficiently inelastic.

1.6 Potential Policy Implications

Assuming the framework above provides a reasonable description of SWF investing behavior, one can construct hypothetical scenarios to analyze potential policy implications to the global economy and its official institutions. Chapter 4 will discuss several such scenarios in detail. In this section, we put one such scenario in the context of a real-world financial development.

What if some monetary institutions are at the brink of collapse, and the general public begin to lose faith in their currencies? There are no lack of historical examples of the public questioning the legitimacy of a "legal tender" or a close substitute, from the Military Yen issued by Japan in occupied territories during the Second World War to the IOUs issued by the State of California during its budget crisis of 2009.

One emerging possibility is that, in the absence of an ever growing supply of precious metals, "currency refugees" may seek refuge in a digital currency that is not backed by any official institution. In fact, one such digital currency, the "bitcoin", experienced dramatic surges in its value after the Cypriot financial crises[11]. Originally a nascent technology experiment, bitcoin is fast gaining acceptance by a number of retail outlets such as coffee shops in San Francisco as a form of payment, with its current circulation reaching close to US$1 billion. The acceptance of such a digital currency has resulted in the following changes in the real economy:

(1) No open and transparent government(s) can effectively stop two private citizens from agreeing to set the price of a cup of coffee to say one bitcoin as long as the transaction's ultimate settlement is conducted via a legal tender;

(2) When willing buyers and sellers in the public both accept that the price for a nice cup of coffee in downtown San Francisco should be one bitcoin (and in the absence of any dramatic changes to the cost of running a coffee shop), inflation in its traditional sense will gradually become a legacy of the past and may even disappear altogether, provided that there are no artificial restrictions on the digital currency's "money supply"; and

(3) Convenient settlement can be done via internet payment services, with many already in existence today. In the future, a global traveler may simply need to fill his or her digital wallet with bitcoins instead of paying for the services of money changers at airports and train stations.

There are several reasons why this new state of affairs can only be achieved via recent technologies. Today, one can buy or sell just about any new or used items over the internet — literally from automobiles to zinc alloys — via websites in major countries and ship the items to most destinations around the world with accessible transportation. Major buyers and sellers on non-US websites often

---

[11]Matt Egan, "As Cyprus Implodes, Bitcoin Interest Explodes", *FOX Business*, 22 March, 2013, http://www.foxbusiness.com/investing/2013/03/22/bitcoin-interest-explodes-as-cyprus-nearly-implodes/#ixzz2PF4gjItW.

accept multiple settlement currencies. Once the digital economy has achieved its current level of convenience and public acceptance, supporting any alternative settlement currency should be relatively straightforward. Second, the widespread availability of smart mobile phones has made it feasible to make instant payments at any retail outlets using digital wallets installed on such devices. Finally, if someone had come up with such a digital currency technology before the financial crisis of 2008, there would have been a real possibility for monetary authorities around the world to stop the adoption of any digital currency or at least keep it as a technology experiment. However, monetary authorities around the world had far more urgent problems to attend to after the 2008 financial crisis. Now that the genie is out of the bottle, it would be far more difficult for any official institutions to reverse the trend.

The potential policy implications to both SWF investors and the global economy are as follows:

(1) Even if certain monetary institutions are at the brink of collapse, some parts of the world can simply revert to either a barter system or a primitive medium of exchange via precious metals, which may create a negative impact on growth due to the lack of flexibility in such a monetary base. With technology, there is now another feasible alternative. Both recent and historical events have shown that the most important qualification of any medium of exchange is not its issuance and backing by any official institution, but rather its public trust and acceptance.

(2) Bitcoin started as a nascent technology experiment so its money supply was set to an artificial ceiling; some commentators have noted this as its critical design flaw[12]. What if a successor crypto-currency will be issued and destroyed based on current and future transactions — as in such "new" bitcoins are created as and when an employee is willing to set aside from his or her monthly pay check an equivalent amount that pays for 100 cups of coffee for future consumption? The monetary base will then be scaled according to actual and future transactions that take place around the world by a smart algorithmic "central bank", and any money supply will then become a true measure of current economic activities and wealth accumulation.

(3) A digital currency will transcend any national border as long as key creditors are willing to accept it as a form of payment.

---

[12]Pascal-Emmanuel Gobry, "This 1998 Paul Krugman Column Perfectly Explains The Design Flaw At The Heart Of Bitcoin", *Forbes*, 5 April, 2013, http://www.forbes.com/sites/ pascalemmanuelgobry/2013/04/05/krugman-baby-sitting-co-op-bitcoin/?utm_ campaign=forbestwittersf&utm_source=twitter&utm_medium=social.

(4) A digital currency is unlikely to replace any national currency soon. However, the idea of a creditor currency union as described in the last section is not completely far-fetched: BRICS countries are already forming its own development bank, which may play certain monetary role in future[13]. Eventually, surplus country SWFs can get together and "coerce" deficit countries to convert their debts into those denominated in a new common currency deemed acceptable by the key creditors.

Deficit countries may have few other choices, unless they have another way to roll over their existing debts. If the surplus countries are keen to form a *de facto* currency union, they are likely to do so initially by essentially pegging to a leading surplus country currency (such as linking to a currency basket dominated by the Chinese yuan) before forming a formal monetary union among surplus countries.

Recent events have shown that the problem with forming a monetary union based on a basket of currencies is that there may be no simple way to let any country that mismanages its public finances exit such a union. A widely accepted digital currency (potentially one issued with the support of a creditor government) works around such a problem by providing an alternative reference to creditor countries, because their key criteria is that the debtor countries will be able to repay their debts in any currency that translates into real purchasing power.

(5) If there is a widely-accepted digital currency that is not directly issued or controlled by any official institution, global markets may evolve in the following ways:

- Tracing money laundering may become easier given digital signatures, but no digital currency will deter a group of determined financial terrorists sponsored by "rogue states";
- The bread-and-butter payment system in commercial banking will eventually be decentralized into a diverse group of payment processors, reducing the risk of "too big to fail" in the banking system; and
- It will be trickier for any debtor country to issue an almost unlimited amount of debts denominated in its own currency. That will help eliminate a certain degree of global imbalance and eventually slow down the growth in assets directly controlled by official institutions and SWFs.

---

[13]"BRICS nations discuss development bank", *BBC News*, 27 March, 2013, http://www.bbc.co.uk/news/business-21951160.

1.7 Summary

This chapter introduces a new framework to think about SWF investing and the evolving roles of SWFs after the 2008 financial crisis.

SWFs are by-products of significant global imbalances. A likely root cause of the problem is a global monetary system that is pro-cyclical when it is supposed to self-correct.

Our proposed model allows researchers to think logically about SWF investing behavior and potential policy implications to the global economy. For instance, in order for SWFs to participate in any financial rescues during a market crisis, the general pre-condition should be that the situation is a liquidity situation, not a solvency crisis. It also does not help if the initial losses expected to be absorbed by the participating SWFs are so huge that it may destabilize or even topple governments.

Any real-world implementation of our proposed model is likely to go beyond SWF investing to incorporate other macro drivers in the global economy, such as open market operations conducted by central banks and government fiscal policies. One can then construct hypothetical scenarios to better understand how SWFs may wish to respond under financial crisis scenarios.

Ultimately, the emergence of large pockets of wealth controlled by official institutions may lead to global financial reforms that would not be possible without a creditor's alliance formed by major surplus countries. History has shown that such rescues typically took place within very short and intense periods of negotiations. Therefore, it is helpful for researchers to "game out" the plausible responses ahead of presenting any action plan proposals, and to undertake reasonable efforts in educating the public ahead of any potential crisis, instead of shocking them with painful medicine in the midst of an unfolding crisis.

Poorly-executed attempts to intervene can make a bad situation worse: If an intervention by SWFs cannot stem the crisis of public trust, the net effect is for these SWFs to lock in more losses by raising cash in a falling market, thereby using up "dry powders" to launch credible rescue attempts subsequently and therefore shaking up market confidence even further.

The rest of this book is organized to expand on the overview presented by this chapter. Chapter 2 will give the context of our discussion by providing a relatively factual description of SWFs and their existing activities. Chapter 3 will describe the main model. Chapter 4 will elaborate on the investment policy implications of such a model. Chapter 5 will conclude.

Chapter 2

Past Realities

2.1 Brief History of Sovereign Wealth Management

After the 2008 global financial crisis, many began to write about Asia emerging as a financial powerhouse, with Asian SWFs playing a particularly prominent role in the global financial stage. As one example, the 2010 Joint ADB-Earth Institute Report [Sachs, Kawai, Lee & Woo (2010)] has identified a number of regional issues associated with the rise of Asia. This chapter attempts to better understand the rise of these predominantly East Asian and Middle Eastern institutions against this sea change in the global financial landscape.

2.1.1 *General Landscape*

The International Monetary Fund (IMF) has identified five types of SWFs that can be distinguished based on their objectives[1]:

(1) *Stabilization funds* — where the primary objective is to insulate the budget and the economy against commodity (usually crude oil) price swings;
(2) *Savings funds for future generations* — which aim to convert non-renewable assets into a more diversified portfolio of assets and mitigate the effects of Dutch disease;
(3) *Reserve investment corporations* — whose assets are often still counted as reserve assets, and are established to increase the return on reserves;

Section 2.1 is the author's own summary of Lee, B. and H. Wang, "Reevaluating the Roles of Large Public Surpluses and Sovereign Wealth Funds in Asia," Tokyo, Japan: Asian Development Bank Institute Working Paper, 2011. Printed with permission from Dr. Wang. Her contributions to the ADBI Working Paper are gratefully acknowledged.
[1]International Monetary Fund, "Sovereign Wealth Funds — A Work Agenda", 29 February, 2008, available from http://www.imf.org/external/np/pp/eng/2008/022908.pdf.

(4) *Development funds* — which typically help fund socio-economic projects or promote industrial policies that might raise a country's potential output growth; and

(5) *Contingent pension reserve funds* — which provide (from sources other than individual pension contributions) for contingent unspecified pension liabilities on the government's balance sheet.

Out of these, the Saving Funds and the Reserve Investment Corporations formats are the most common. In practice, SWFs are rarely "purist" and usually serve a mix of objectives. Some countries are also known to deploy multiple sovereign investment vehicles with each having a different investment focus.

2.1.2   *Excess Reserve Accumulation*

We seek to better understand the historical reasons for the accumulation of large public surpluses. The excess reserves from these large public surpluses are the assets managed by SWFs.

Saving Funds are typically by-products of natural history and geology: Saving Fund is a mechanism to diversify national wealth away from any over-concentration of national wealth in minerals. The goal is to manage such wealth in an endowment format to benefit multiple future generations and to avoid the infamous Dutch disease[2]. The typical size of a Saving Fund is directly proportional to a nation's endowment of mineral wealth.

Reserve Investment Corporations are intellectually more interesting to think about. Under perfectly efficient foreign exchange markets, a standard assumption made by the classical theories of comparative advantage in international economics, no country should experience persistent trade surpluses and therefore enjoy any opportunity to build up ever-growing reserves. An exporter's goods and services will eventually become more expensive due to the demands on its currencies by its importers. At the same time, an importer's domestic goods become cheaper due to currency depreciation, or the exporter may choose to relocate production activities to importer countries to take advantage of lower costs. Such currency flows and subsequent adjustments will roughly equalize the price of goods produced in different countries over time. Based on the logic above, the

---

[2]The "Dutch disease" is a term coined by *The Economist* in the 70's to describe the decline of the Dutch manufacturing sector after the discovery of the largest European natural gas field in Groningen. The term is used to describe the apparent relationship between the exploitation of national resources and a decline in the manufacturing and/or agriculture sector(s). Revenues from natural resources lead to a surge in price levels, making exports more expensive and leading to a decline of manufacturing. See "The Dutch Disease", *The Economist*, 26 November, 1977, pp. 82–83.

most likely explanation of persistent trade imbalance is the structural inflexibility found in some segments of the global exchange rate regime.

Let's conduct the following thought experiment: The world has reasonably efficient foreign exchange markets with no capital control restrictions. Exporters can invest their trade surpluses into assets located inside importers or sold by those importers. Put differently, importers pay for their imports by selling assets. Eventually, an exporter's trade surpluses will be offset by its investment outflows, and vice versa for an importer's trade deficits. There is no apparent reason why there should be persistent accumulation of official reserves over a sufficiently long period that will allow the appropriate adjustments to take place.

Moreover, it is not obvious why the scenario above should be considered "undesirable" when importing countries are typically populated by greying populations. Of course, we assume that domestic investors are capable of making sophisticated international investments, and that the domestic government still has sufficient precautionary excess reserves to safeguard its national balance sheet. How, then, is our world today deviating from this simple thought experiment, leading to the persistent accumulation of public surpluses and significant distortions in global balances of trade and payments? Can inefficient and inflexible foreign exchange markets alone explain the observed outcomes? Are there any other reasons for market mechanisms to fail persistently to self-correct? With SWFs being a phenomena among primarily East Asian and Middle Eastern countries, why are such failures more commonly observed in those parts of the world only?

2.1.3 *"Free" Market Capitalism*

In a lighthearted bestseller written by a Cambridge don, Chang (2010) argues that free-market capitalism has created many of the problems seen in today's global economies. Likewise, Stiglitz *et al.* (2006) suggest that structural policies, such as capital market liberalization, are blunt policy instruments. They have often been implemented with unfavorable outcomes for economic stability and long-term growth among developing countries. These prominent economists essentially point to the lack of empirical evidence supporting that the type of "free" market capitalism often advocated in textbooks can create sustainable growth and economic well-being for mankind.

In short, no short-term public policy changes can correct the phenomenon of persistent global imbalance. In the absence of an overnight policy solution, we must be prepared to deal with the longer-term consequences of persistent global imbalances. One practical consequence is that these imbalances have allowed certain Western governments to keep running large fiscal deficits. In addition, since many Asian countries still remember the traumas from the Asian financial crisis in the late 90's, some have taken the extreme precaution of accumulating huge amounts of "rainy day" public surpluses, even after Asian foreign exchange markets have since become more efficient. It is fair to ask how much is enough, and whether the relevant Asian governments are creating more problems instead of solving known ones by accumulating reserves significantly beyond what may be reasonable for defensive purposes.

Let's conduct another thought experiment. Imagine a world in which every country agrees to print an "extra" pool of domestic currencies in exchange for similar "extra" foreign currencies printed by other countries. This way, every country can build up an artificial official reserve that can be used by central banks to facilitate day-to-day cross-border settlements. As long as these pools are kept away from general circulation, there is no logical reason to rush into any conclusion that an artificial arrangement in which central banks are exchanging foreign currencies with each other will create inflationary problems. In fact, a "virtual" form of such an artificial arrangement exists today, in which the practical operational size of any such bilateral swap facility is determined empirically by the net settlement of day-to-day transactions[3].

The real problem with the simplistic thought experiment as described above is that some debtor governments may decide to use the money raised from the selling of bonds to other central banks to finance massive fiscal deficits. That is in effect equivalent to one country in this model "selling down" its foreign exchange reserves unilaterally. Doing so can result in monetary expansion in the real economy of that country. In that case, all other countries will end up with a higher-than-warranted allocation of that country's currency in their respective pools. In addition, the net saver countries in the model may also decide to use their reserves to invest in tangible assets instead of holding government bonds. As a result, the pools in the model above become an increasingly significant part of the real economy. Obviously, there are always temptations for countries in fiscal difficulties to "sell down" their pools of foreign exchange reserves; the practical question is at which point these economies will begin to face the real risk of self-inflicting the Dutch disease.

At the end of the day, there may be some natural and logical reasons for every major region of the world to maintain a pool of official reserves in currencies outside its own. The recent Greek and Cypriot crises have shown that the euro does not yet offer a credible alternative to the United States (US) dollar as a reserve

---

[3]Please refer to http://www.mas.gov.sg/news_room/press_releases/2010/MAS_and_PBC_bilateral_currency_swap.html for one example of a bilateral currency swap facility between the People's Bank of China and the Monetary Authority of Singapore.

currency. Unless Asian countries begin to use a currency created by an Asian monetary union or even an artificial basket of Asian currencies as the region's anchor currency, it is far from clear what other dependable alternatives there are for central banks around the world to stop using the US dollar as their primary store of value. Another practical issue with the simplistic thought experiment discussed above is that there is no credible Asian currency or basket for non-Asian central banks to hold, while Asian countries are basically "stuck" with using the US dollar as their primary base currency to store value. As a consequence, the one-way build-up of massive US dollar-dominated public surpluses in Asia will remain an economic fact of life in the foreseeable future.

2.1.4 *Rescuer of Last Resort*

At the height of the 2008 financial crisis, a few prominent Western financial institutions at the risk of collapsing sought help from Asian official institutions to finance their rescue packages. Estimates on the total amount of recapitalization required to restore the global financial system to its pre-Basel-II state of health are roughly in the trillion-dollar range [Lee (2009)]. Given that only the Asian official institutions will have balance sheets large enough to supply such an astronomical amount of capital, they are expected to play a possible role in restoring the health of the global financial system.

There are practical advantages in defining such roles for Asian official institutions, as well as the potential responsibilities and obligations involved. It is almost impossible for any rescuer to time its intervention at the precise bottom of a collapsing stock market. The public is also not known for making charitable comparison to the proverbial alternative of "doing nothing", so the ensuing market volatility often leads to public outcry on the "misuse" of public coffers by the rescuers. By educating the public in advance, there is a better chance that governments will not be forced by public opinions to reverse course in the midst of launching a rescue operation, even when such a rescue is the right path to pursue. In addition, certain basic criteria can be established way ahead of any crisis scenario: Unlike the IMF Executive Board with a pre-agreed upon voting procedure, a collection of independent Asian official institutions may not all agree on how best to make certain difficult choices between moral hazard and long-term economic malaise in a time of crisis.

From an institutional perspective, there are also pragmatic reasons for Asian SWFs to better define their *de facto* role as the global rescuer of last resort, beyond their common role of providing fiscal stability for their own domestic economies. In the next section, we will refer to research suggesting limited evidence of alpha or firm-specific returns available to SWFs; their returns are thought to be driven primarily by beta or asset allocation. A SWF also cannot engage in typical trading-oriented hedging activities because the notional amount that they will be required to take short positions in may be large enough to cause the very market crash that they are hoping to avoid, thereby defeating the original purpose of the hedge. As a result, one pragmatic "tail risk" hedging technique that can be pursued by a SWF is to act as the global rescuer of last resort, by guiding the global economy away from any potential collapse. To them, financing rescues as a "tail risk" hedge is still a better alternative than holding potentially worthless pieces of IOUs when issuers go default. Typically, net-saver countries have no interest in creating any situation in which their main customers will stop buying their goods and services, at least not before there is a fair chance for the appropriate adjustments to be made; instead, their focus tends to be on ensuring that they can collect payments or seize the appropriate collaterals from such customers.

In other words, it is conceivable for mega-sized, public investors in Asia to play a stabilizing role for the global financial system. In fact, Hu Xiaolian, former Deputy Governor of the People's Bank of China, the People's Republic of China's (PRC) central bank, proposed the possible creation of a "superfund" with dual market stabilization and profit-seeking objectives[4]. Although that type of structure may allow Asian official institutions to herald the reform of financial markets and their regulations, many have good reasons to be wary of its potential domination by one single country or a handful of countries. Nonetheless, the recognition that something ought to be done regardless of how is an important first step.

2.1.5   *Alpha and Size*

Berk & Green (2004) suggested that there is a natural limit on the type of excess returns that can be delivered by active portfolio managers. Their argument is that it is illogical for all investors to generate "above average" excess returns, since the aggregate set of all investors represents the market. Based on that logic, the "mining" of alpha by active managers will become increasingly difficult, as assets flow into an out-performing asset class, or as the investors become increasingly bigger in size.

There is in fact empirical evidence supporting the theoretic arguments given by Berk & Green (2004). Fung *et al.* (2008) found no detectable alpha by analyzing funds-of-hedge-funds data over a ten-year period from January 1995 to December

---

[4]See Christopher Anstey, "PBOC's Hu Sees Multinational Sovereign Wealth Fund", *Bloomberg News*, 22 September, 2009. Actual text of the proposal can be found on the G20 website http://www.g20.org.

2004, during which hedge funds as an asset class attracted explosive growth. Consistent with the predictions in Berk & Green (2004), large capital inflows into a fund resulted in lower alpha as well as negative impact on alpha persistence. Estimated net alpha received by investors also decreased. These observations support the hypothesis of a finite amount of alpha available to all investors. The lesson learned is that perhaps investors at the size of SWFs should avoid hedge funds, particularly the trading-oriented ones.

In addition, Ang, Goetzmann & Schaefer (2009) found that the Norwegian SWF showed practically no active return. This observation supports the hypothesis that it is difficult for very large portfolios to achieve active returns due to their size. Similarly, earlier statistical research done by Lee & Lee (2004b) showed that the net performance of any funds of hedge funds will become unexciting, as increasingly bigger investors can only invest in more and more hedge funds due to capacity constraints. A possible explanation is that the end investor will end up with a portfolio of many hedge funds each taking canceling long and short positions in the same underlying security universe of investable securities, limiting the end investor's ability to achieve impressive returns.

These observations are important to SWFs. Massive AUM can limit the ability for a SWF to benefit from active portfolio management. SWFs may be better off by trying to generate returns from one or more of the following sources:

(1) asset allocation;
(2) strategic sectors that naturally complement a country's national balance sheet; and/or
(3) specialized "alpha" investments such as private equity or venture capital deals.

2.1.6 *Non-Investment Considerations*

Whether the amount of Asian official reserves is sufficient in the post-crisis period remains an open question. Moreover, readers should note that only a handful of Asian countries have reserves large enough to invest the excess amount (over and above what is necessary for precautionary purposes) in SWFs, which typically aim for higher returns than government bond yields by investing in "non-risk-free" assets. Finally, many of these SWFs experienced dramatic drawdowns and then subsequent bounce-backs. Some SWFs learned the hard way that there could be heavy political costs when facing massive drawdowns, regardless of whether the drawdowns were within expectations, and whether the SWFs were successful in recovering from the drawdowns in subsequent reporting periods.

In the run-up to the Financial Crisis, one likely key factor contributing to significant surpluses/deficits in the global balance of payments is inflexible exchange rate policy. The persistent imbalance has in turn allowed certain countries to run unsustainable fiscal policies. The resulting negative feedback cycle may have gone too far and for too long, to allow effective correction by monetary policies and other relevant forms of policy cooperation. In a way, the very existence of SWFs is a by-product of this seemingly unhealthy phenomenon.

The pragmatic issue is how one can practically get out of this quagmire. In order to make the necessary adjustments to the global balance of payments, ultimately there must be a viable alternative to what has been a regime of effectively pegged currencies in Asia. That is particularly true for the PRC. Even a hint of slowing down in its purchase of an ever-growing stockpile of US Treasuries can send US Treasury prices tumbling. This situation cannot be sustained forever without a potential debasement of the US dollar, which is hardly in the interest of the US or that of the PRC. If it can be problematic to even suggest a potential decrease in the total amount of official reserves, perhaps a smarter alternative is to begin taking some of the excess official reserves (i.e. above and beyond what will be reasonably needed for precautionary purposes) to invest in certain strategic growth sectors, and to acquire hard assets overseas instead of letting the stockpile of Western government debts grow in perpetuity. That is likely to mean enlarging the roles of SWFs in managing Asia's total excess official reserves.

In the post-Crisis era, another key question faced by SWFs is what risk is really manageable and/or hedgeable for any outsized net exporter of capital? How does one maintain the values of assets denominated in currencies with potential risk of debasement? Also, is there any practical solution to address the economic, financial and political implications of massive foreign exchange hedging transactions? If it is not feasible for Asian institutions to rely on playing defense, then perhaps the practical alternative is for them to play offense, by looking for allocation policies that will maximize the possibility of stimulating global growth and therefore economic recovery. Ultimately, only when a credible Asian alternative reserve currency is available, Asian public surpluses can be invested in Asian assets instead of Western government bonds as one way to restore the global balance of payments. That calls for Asian SWFs playing a role in the growth and development of not just Asian financial markets but Asian economies in general.

2.2 Factors Impacting Investing Behavior

2.2.1 *Assets Under Management*

Figure 2.1 shows a pie chart that describes the distribution of sovereign wealth assets under management (AUM) as reported by the Sovereign Wealth Fund Institute on *Wikipedia*[5]. Out of the total of US$5.4 trillion reported, mineral funds account for approximately 59% of reported assets under management, while non-mineral funds account for 41%. These reported statistics are not expected to give an extremely accurate representation of reality, since China is quite likely to be undercounted in its overall share of the total. There is not yet full transparency on how China's State Administration of Foreign Exchange (SAFE) manages its over US$3 trillion in foreign exchange reserves, as well as how much of its non-fixed income investments are counted as sovereign wealth investments.

Figure 2.2 shows that the top-five mineral fund sponsor countries are Norway, United Arab Emirates, Saudi Arabia, Kuwait and Russia. Figure 2.3 shows that the top-5 non-mineral fund sponsoring countries are China, Hong Kong, Singapore, Australia and South Korea. Moreover, the wealth concentration is extreme: After the top-five countries, most other countries barely have 1 or 2% of the total pie. The top-11 funds in both mineral and non-mineral funds exceed 80% of the total AUM at US$4.3 trillion. While the average fund size among the top-11 funds is an impressive US$389 billion, the average among all other funds (excluding the unreported sub-US$100 million category) is just US$21 billion, which is comparable to the size of a typical pension plan. The ratio of these two categories is more than 18 times.

Clearly, the SWFs that are interesting to study are the top funds accounting for most of the reported assets. The massive size of these SWFs creates two potential investment issues:

(1) Whether there may be too many large SWFs globally and/or they may be too big (as a percentage of total global wealth) to create the possibility of Dutch disease. Even if their proceeds are invested outside of their home countries, the money will eventually find ways to flow back to surplus countries in today's global business environment, in which it is generally difficult to invest in multinational corporations that exclude doing business in specific countries. There may also be a policy need to define a recommended level of official reserves required for precautionary needs, beyond which only the excess should be invested in a SWF.

---

[5]See http://en.wikipedia.org/wiki/Sovereign_wealth_fund.

(2) If there are too many SWFs and/or they are too big, eventually the net flow into investable instruments will erode the aggregated returns (the total amount of economic rents due to aggregated global economic activities) available to everyone simply by artificially "buying up" the valuation in any one particular market segment. One may argue that this is not necessarily true based on the successful track records of certain large SWFs, such as the Government of Singapore Investment Corporation (GIC) and Temasek Holdings (TH). They have proven their abilities to produce returns that are competitive to their smaller counterparts. In addition, one should not automatically assume that investment inflows by SWFs will drive down alpha. Their investments are often of such sizes that, if their holdings work out, the returns will lift entire economies and markets, and therefore the typical liquid market benchmarks will benefit as well. So, the real issue here may be the lack of an appropriate choice of performance benchmark for SWFs.

2.2.2 *Investment Objectives and Performance Benchmarks*

Before the 2008 financial crisis, there was a trend among SWFs (with the majority of them starting in the 90's, as relatively "young" operations) to essentially imitate trillion-dollar-sized commercial fund managers. In fact, some SWFs were known to kick start their organizations by hiring senior professionals from those commercial fund managers.

During the 2008 financial crisis, certain SWFs found out the hard way that their investment strategies might not have fully considered low-probability but high-impact tail risk events such as the financial crisis itself. Unlike commercial operators, SWFs began to realize that their asset management strategies and risk management techniques ought to accommodate the remote possibility that they might be required by their sponsoring governments to respond to macro and systematic events.

After the 2008 financial crisis, technocratic Western governments no longer show knee-jerk hostility toward foreign government ownership, without such emergency investments their own banking systems might have collapsed. At the same time, there was a change in the way by which some SWFs ran their day-to-day operations: e.g. collateral management became a key concern once SWFs realized that cash deposited at Western banking institutions might turn into substantially discounted general obligations, in the event of any systematic banking collapse.

Let's examine the appropriate investment objectives and choice of performance benchmarks for the two main categories of SWFs:

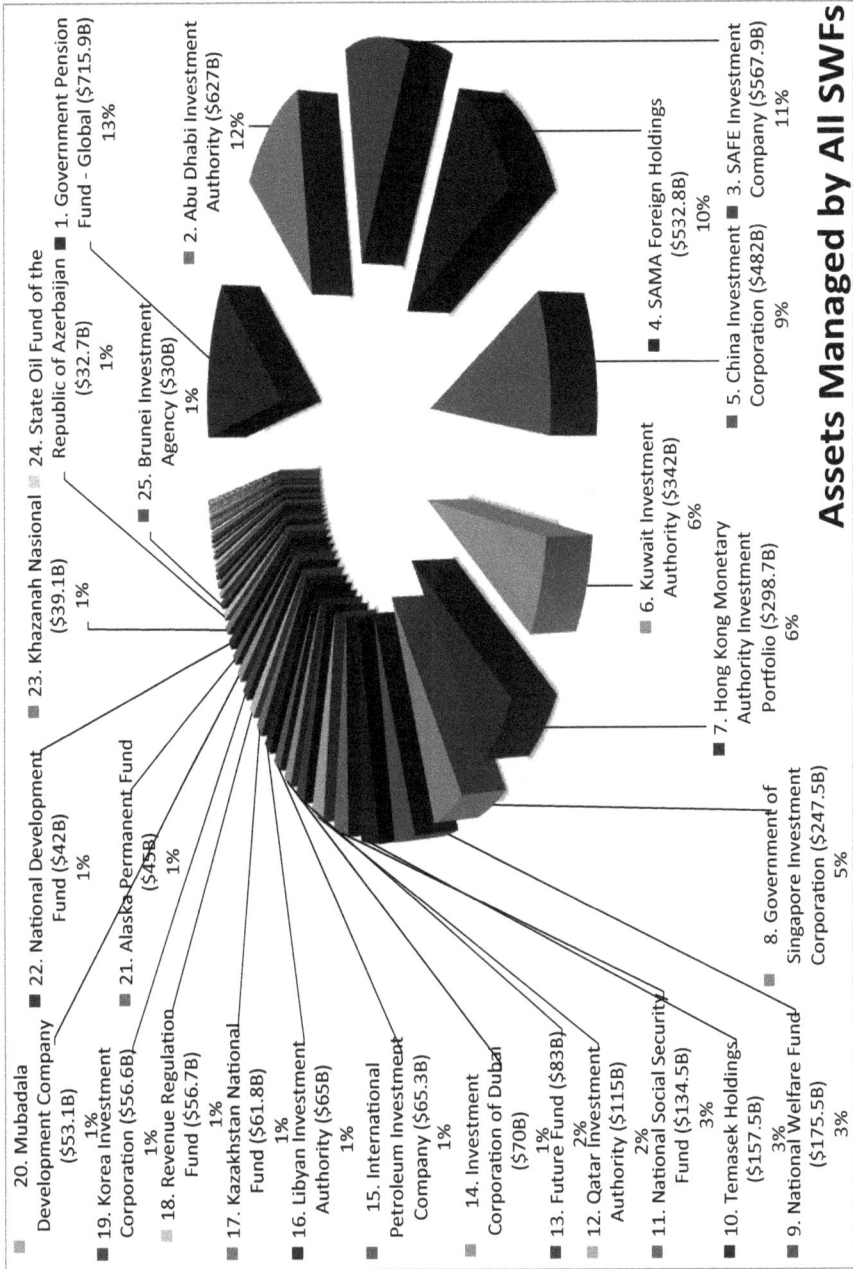

Fig. 2.1 Assets Under Management for All SWFs

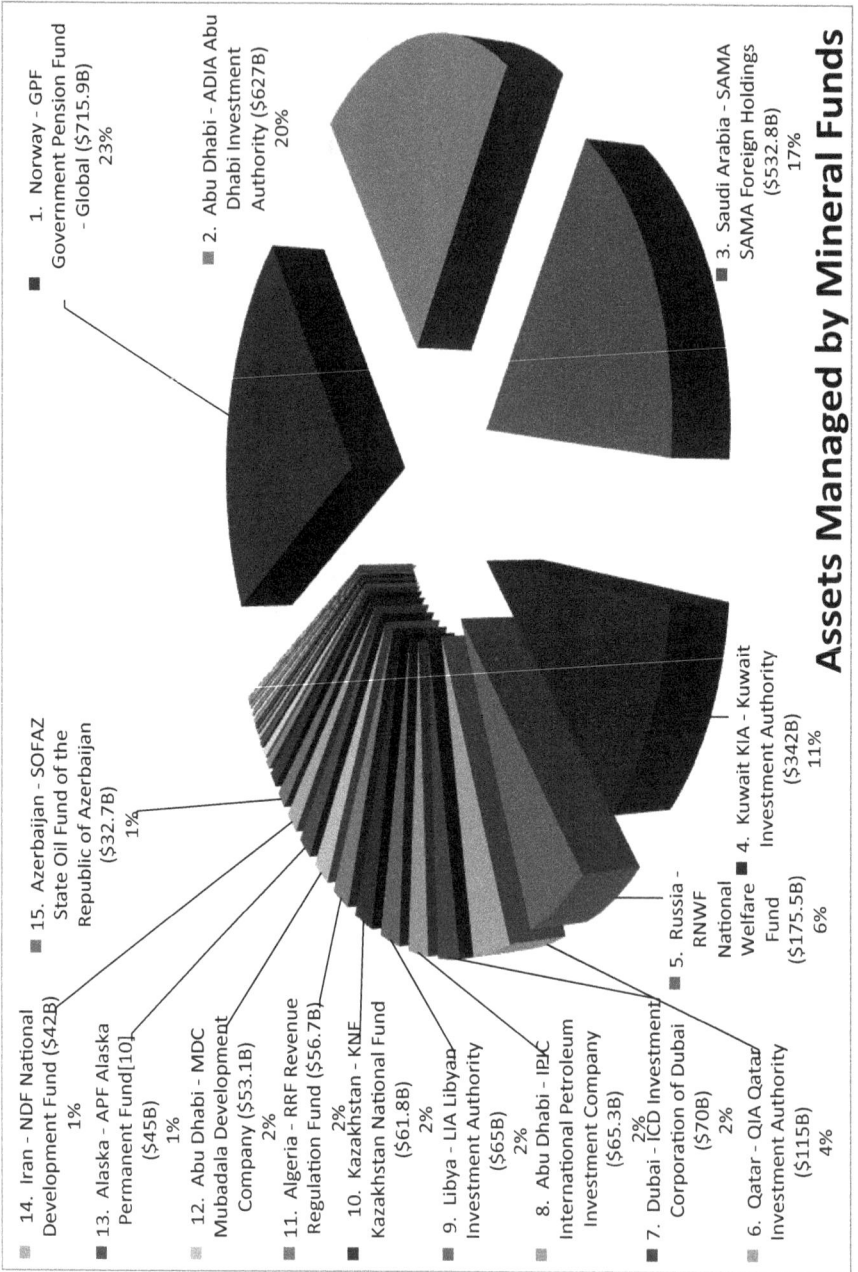

Assets Managed by Mineral Funds

- 1. Norway - GPF Government Pension Fund - Global ($715.9B) 23%
- 2. Abu Dhabi - ADIA Abu Dhabi Investment Authority ($627B) 20%
- 3. Saudi Arabia - SAMA SAMA Foreign Holdings ($532.8B) 17%
- 4. Kuwait KIA - Kuwait Investment Authority ($342B) 11%
- 5. Russia - RNWF National Welfare Fund ($175.5B) 6%
- 6. Qatar - QIA Qatar Investment Authority ($115B) 4%
- 7. Dubai - ICD Investment Corporation of Dubai ($70B) 2%
- 8. Abu Dhabi - IPIC International Petroleum Investment Company ($65.3B) 2%
- 9. Libya - LIA Libyan Investment Authority ($65B) 2%
- 10. Kazakhstan - KNF Kazakhstan National Fund ($61.8B) 2%
- 11. Algeria - RRF Revenue Regulation Fund ($56.7B) 2%
- 12. Abu Dhabi - MDC Mubadala Development Company ($53.1B) 2%
- 13. Alaska - APF Alaska Permanent Fund[10] ($45B) 1%
- 14. Iran - NDF National Development Fund ($42B) 1%
- 15. Azerbaijan - SOFAZ State Oil Fund of the Republic of Azerbaijan ($32.7B) 1%

Fig. 2.2   Assets Under Management for Mineral Funds

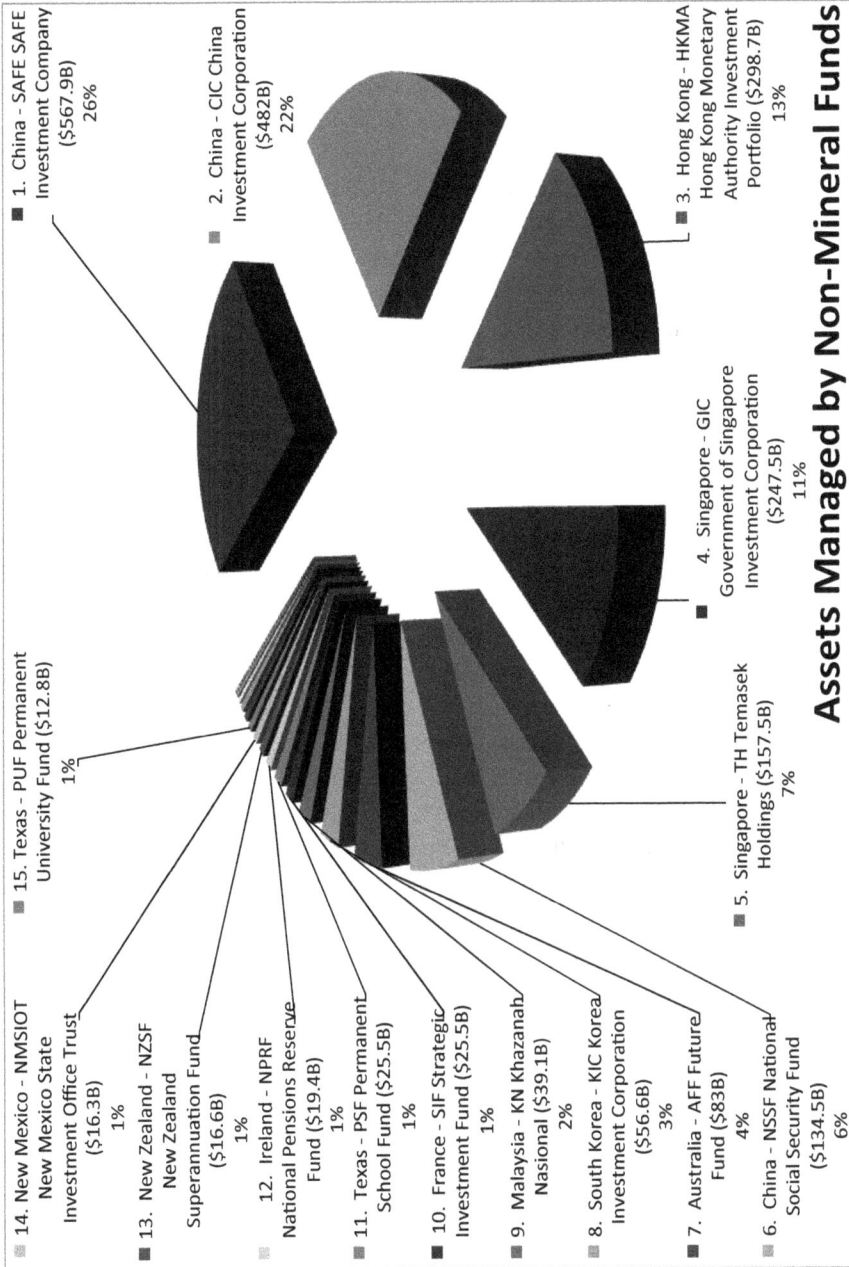

Fig. 2.3   Assets Under Management for Non-Mineral Funds

(1) *Mineral Funds* — Their general investment objective is to diversify national wealth from mineral-driven receipts, also known as revenue regulation. Ideally, this is implemented by producing absolute returns that are either uncorrelated or negatively correlated to price fluctuations in the commodity markets. However, one should note that there are no practical ways to go "long-short" in typical SWFs, when the notional size required to hedge out any SWF factor exposures often exceeds any practical tradeable amounts relative to liquid markets. The only way to reliably achieve absolute returns is by investing in certificates of deposit, since even fixed income investments may suffer significant capital losses in times of crisis. In practice, most mineral funds aim to invest in a variety of diversified asset classes, including some with irregular mark-to-market values. That way, if the mineral wealth does run out one day, or if the endowed minerals are no longer in strong demands globally, there will be sufficient financial wealth left to support multiple generations.

Typical liquid market benchmarks are designed for assessing the performance of commercial asset management operations. However, SWF balance sheet characteristics are different from those of commercial operators. For instance, a mineral fund may consider investing in timber and rare earth metals to complement an endowed wealth portfolio consisted of petrochemicals and base metals. Such an investment strategy can result in a form of national self-sufficiency when one day the world may no longer enjoy relatively unrestricted global commerce seen in the time of plenty. However, most commercial benchmarks only contain liquid commodity tradeables. In particular, rare earth metals are generally illiquid due to their relatively low volumes traded, while timber is not widely traded in open exchanges due to varying grades and species. As a result, it is difficult to come up with any objective performance benchmark for such an asset allocation. A naïve measure of out-performance relative to the yields of government bonds or certificates of deposit may result in extreme short-term out-performance only to be followed by intense disappointment.

(2) *Non-Mineral Funds* — Their general goal is to "pick" investments to complement their national balance sheets. For instance, Temasek Holdings in Singapore is well known for investing in strategic industries to complement the city-state's open economy. Similarly, China was explicit about gaining private equity investment expertise by investing in Blackstone. It can also be argued that at least part of China's massive infrastructure spending should be counted as part of its SWF portfolio; as an example, it is not obvious whether it is appropriate to split China's construction of an inter-continental high-speed rail

network into domestic and SWF investments by a simple geographical cost allocation.

The challenge in benchmarking their performance is that their portfolios often consist of many hard-to-value, illiquid private investments. These investments exhibit idiosyncratic risks and characteristics, with no reliable valuations feasible until there are viable exits. When successful, such investments may turn into significant portions of the investee countries' market indices, thus driving the valuations of securities in entire regions or sectors. One classic investment example is that of a hydroelectric dam. A successful investment may end up driving industrial development for an entire economic region, without showing significant out-performance relative to a benchmark containing components that represent such an economy. Such an investment in effect drives the benchmark instead of any "alpha" alone.

Since the 2008 financial crisis, the need to measure SWF performance as a potential liquidity provider in distressed scenarios begins to emerge. Using a set of performance measures similar to those for commercial operators, such as out-performance against traditional liquid market benchmarks, does not capture any such information. For instance, a SWF that is inclined to invest in assets with no regular mark to market (and therefore artificially low "observable" volatility) may look attractive in stable markets but may represent a poor liquidity buffer, because such assets are highly unlikely to be liquidated or widely accepted as collateral in most crisis scenarios. Simply showing out-performance relative to traditional liquid market benchmarks may be grossly misleading.

2.2.3 *Constraints and Regulations*

Although technocratic Western governments no longer show knee-jerk hostility toward foreign government ownership after the 2008 financial crisis, various forms of protectionism are far from subsiding. Both the US and European Union have become more active with anti-dumping duties in recent years, imposed on such items as Chinese honey, resulting in a tragicomical wave of "honey laundering." The difficulties and costs involved in enforcement actions have not been effective against the total amount of tariffs collectable. A non-protectionist and rational US government would have avoided creating any such irritant when the US-China trade imbalances were US$315 billion in 2012 and US$69 billion within just the first three months of 2013, with most of the surpluses ending up in US Treasuries and related US-Government-linked securities.

Why would any country pick a fight with its banker over something that is seemingly so trivial? What if the surplus countries refuse to continue lending just to roll over the debtor's existing debts? The fact is, just within the first quarter of 2013, the Chinese had foreign direct investment (FDI) inflow of US$29.9 billion, while its FDI outflow was US$23.8 billion[6]. With more inflow than outflow despite large trade surpluses, the main problem for China as well as similar surplus countries is that they do not have too many viable alternatives to recycle their surpluses. In fact, the majority of US Treasuries bought by foreign governments are now held by exporters[7]. If these exporters stop shipping their exports, their domestic economies will suffer from pervasive loss of jobs; receiving IOU's for exports is still a more promising alternative. By comparison, mineral exporters tend to be able to avoid such headaches since their bargaining position is demand-driven[8].

2.2.3.1   *Investment Constraints*

Many Western countries require "national security" reviews prior to the approval of investments by foreign government controlled entities. The most often cited example of such review boards is the Committee on Foreign Investment in the United States (CFIUS). In Australia, similar reviews are conducted by the Foreign Investment Review Board (FIRB). In Canada, they are done under the Investment Canada Act. As our final example, Germany requires parliamentary approval for any foreign investments that may "endanger national interests."

(1) Initially, this type of review mechanism is viewed largely as a way to generate additional fees for law firms and investment banks at investee countries, with perhaps a few notable exceptions such as the case of Dubai World Ports, in which there was indeed a legitimate concern due to the potential links between cargo security and potential acts of terrorism.

(2) As the number of reviews grew, there is increasing evidence that such review mechanisms are driven less by transparent rules but more often by arbitrary political considerations. For instance, the US has never presented credible evidence linking Huawei to Chinese military activities in reviewing its proposed purchases of 3Com and 3Leaf. It only cited that its president once served in

---

[6]See http://www.cnbc.com/id/100651161.

[7]See http://www.treasury.gov/resource-center/data-chart-center/tic/Documents/mfh.txt.

[8]According to the 2011 CFIUS Annual Report (http://www.treasury.gov/resource-center/international/foreign-investment/Documents/2011\%20CFIUS\%20Annual\%20Report\%20FINAL\%20PUBLIC.pdf), oil exporters receive far fewer reviews from CFIUS due to potential investments in the US.

the Chinese People's Liberation Army. Given the large number of US technology companies with senior management members having served in the US military, the natural criticism was whether there were genuine and actionable concerns or simply ill-disguised excuses to protect US technology company Cisco from a fierce foreign competitor?

(3) Finally, the purposes of these reviews are less about serving any traditional definitions of national security, but more often about defining national interests broadly as protecting national economic leadership. As an example, a number of countries are interested in gaining expertise in hydraulic fracturing technologies for shale gas. There is a common understanding in the energy industry that US drillers with the necessary geological expertise are probably not available for sale to any foreign government related entities, presumably due to the shortage of qualified geologists in the US. It is not immediately obvious why hydraulic fracturing technologies should be classified as a national security issue instead of a more traditional national economic leadership issue.

2.2.3.2 *Regulations*

The regulations applicable to SWF investments, in particular their tax treatments, are also dismissed by skeptics as somewhat arbitrary. In general, governments are classified as non-profit entities, which should be considered non-taxable in most developed market tax jurisdictions. However, investee countries in fiscal difficulties are motivated to use SWF investments as opportunities to increase tax revenues. Gradually, investee countries are finding creative ways to tax without discouraging purchase of government bonds by foreign central banks, and thus are seen as imposing hypocritical double standards.

(1) Foreign governments are supposed to be non-profit organizations with reciprocal tax exemptions. After all, taxing gains from government bond investments may be self-defeating, as the issuing entity may simply need to increase yields in bond auctions to the point where investors are willing to accept such yields on an after-tax basis. Governments are also making finer distinction between the integral parts of foreign governments, such as a treasury function, as opposed to "controlled entities", such as SWFs. In addition, certain commercial activities by investee entities may negate tax exemptions.

(2) Each country has its own definition of what should be considered "ill-gotten" gains. In the context of SWFs, usually the concern is not about dealing with proceeds from criminal activities, but more often about reinvesting proceeds from countries under specific international sanctions. As an example, if Iran

agrees to barter its oil for agricultural commodities due to sanctions imposed by the US and European Union, are there legal grounds for freezing Iranian assets purchased from selling bartered agricultural commodities? After all, barter deals are generally seen as humanitarian in nature and are not considered outright violations of international sanctions[9].

(3) Both France and Germany demanded repatriation of their gold reserves from the US for reasons that did not seem to be primarily economically driven. Also, it is not uncommon for assets held by countries caught in civil wars to be frozen and repatriated only to legitimate and recognized post-war governments to minimize the possible use of proceeds to purchase weapons that may harm innocent civilians.

2.3   Risk and Performance Analysis

Next, we seek to better understand both the risk and performance characteristics of specific SWFs. Since we will not be able to analyze every flavor of SWFs available, we have chosen to focus on only the Norwegian Government Pension Fund — Global and Singapore's Temasek Holdings as representatives of these two categories of SWFs:

(1) *Mineral Funds* — Norway is reported to have the largest single mineral fund in the world. Unlike the rest of the top-5 mineral funds, the Norwegian SWF is run by a transparent, elected government, whose investment decisions are less likely to be driven by non-investment reasons, such as *quid pro quo* to the friends and families of any ruling dynasties. These characteristics make it interesting to study the Norwegian SWF as a "control" example of how a mineral fund may be run in the absence of significant non-investment constraints.

(2) *Non-Mineral Funds* — Among the top-5 non-mineral funds, two of them are Singaporean, while the other three are all Chinese-owned. While the Singapore SWF model is widely imitated around the world, China's reserve management behavior tends to be idiosyncratic. This is why it is interesting to study a Singaporean fund; in particular, why study Temasek Holdings instead of the Government of Singapore Investment Corporation? In general, holding information on Temasek Holdings is more readily available from public filings of its large positions, which bear similarities to typical "private equity" positions, but with significant diversification on the remaining 20% of its port-

---

[9]See   http://www.bloomberg.com/news/2012-03-29/india-and-china-skirt-iran-sanctions-with-junk-for-oil-.html.

folios. However, it should be noted that Temasek Holdings does not identify itself as a SWF.

2.3.1 *Return Analysis Example — Norway Government Pension Fund*

Almost by construction, the Norwegian Government Pension Fund — Global (GPFG) portfolio takes minimal active risk given a strategic benchmark composed of 60% in global equities, 35–40% in global fixed income, and 0–5% in global real estate. Thereafter, Norges Bank Investment Management (NBIM, the manager of the GPFG portfolio) adopts an operational benchmark portfolio with significant resemblance to the strategic benchmark, but one that reflects the following additional features[10]:

(1) methodological weaknesses and unnecessary complexity of the strategic benchmark index;
(2) adjustments to the fund's investment universe;
(3) structural changes in the markets;
(4) alternatives to market weighting; and
(5) time-varying risk premiums.

Various independent studies have already shown that GPFG's returns can be attributed primarily to passive returns. One key source of its active returns is caused by a number of excluded companies that fail to adhere to the Ethical Guidelines published by the Norwegian Ministry of Finance. Potential violations that may lead to the removal from GPFG's investment universe include human rights violations, war crimes, environmental damages, gross corruption, and any other violations of current as well as future ethical norms. Most of the exclusions to-date are related to tobacco production, severe environmental damage, production of certain types of munitions, as well as proven human or labor right violations.

> The regulations include an objective to convince businesses to comply with ethical guidelines in the form of "Active Ownership"; exerting (sic) influence in the board room. In the case of non-compliance, the Fund will sell its share and the firm is excluded from the portfolio. Norges Bank is responsible for "Active Ownership", whereas the Ethics Council is responsible for submitting proposals for the exclusion of businesses to the Ministry of Finance. Then, the Ministry of Finance takes the final decision, which up to now has always followed the suggestions of the Ethics Council.[11]

---

[10]See http://www.nbim.no/press-and-publications/feature-articles/2012/use-of-benchmarks-in-the-fund-management/.

[11]This explanation was published by the Center for International Climate and Environmental Research, an independent research center associated with the University of Oslo at

According to the *Financial Times*, given its size of 4.182 trillion Norwegian Kroner (as of 31 March 2013, or US$712.7 billion) as the largest sovereign wealth fund in the world[12], GPFG is expected to reach $1 trillion by the end of the decade. Impressively, GPFG owns an average of 1.25% of every listed company in the world[13].

Upon further analysis, the returns of GPFG can be characterized as follows:

(1) Given the size of the fund, there will be market liquidity issues for GPFG to make any significant active investments. However, investing by strict adherence to market capitalization is known to create the potential problem of buying overvalued stocks and selling undervalued stocks. GPFG may benefit from the emergence of "smart" beta type strategy in which the purchase of shares is not mechanically tied to market capitalization.

(2) A passive investment strategy will work well only when global economy continues to grow. As an example, in any pervasive global recession or even an economic depression, no matter how well diversified a portfolio is run, GPFG is likely to suffer steep losses in all of its asset classes. Since it is well established that wealth creation is driven by innovation in most developed markets[14], a passive investment does not incentivize the wealth creation process, which is a significant issue if *all* SWFs follow a similar strategy. With GPFG's predecessor the Petroleum Fund only established in 1990, it is possible for GPFG's passive investment strategy to have worked well only for the relatively short-term existence of GPFG relative to the history of global capital markets.

(3) Real estate is the one asset class in which the primary practical method to participate in the market is by picking the right assets. Typical real estate assets are marked once a year. Thus, their performance reflects mostly foreign exchange risk during the rest of the year. However, given the small size of this asset class, their impact to GPFG's overall performance is expected to be not significant.

---

http://www.cicero.uio.no/fulltext/index_e.aspx?id=6864. The full text of the Ethical Guidelines as adopted by the Norwegian Ministry of Finance on 1 March 2010 is available from http://www.regjeringen.no/en/sub/styrer-rad-utvalg/ethics_council/ethical-guidelines.html?id=425277.

[12]See http://www.swfinstitute.org/fund-rankings/.

[13]See http://www.ft.com/cms/s/0/a0767042-df40-11e2-a9f4-00144feab7de.html#axzz2Zhqlxnhg.

[14]As an example, of the original 12 stocks that made up the original Dow Jones Industrial Average in 1896, only General Electric remains on today's list. See http://www.forbes.com/sites/steveschaefer/2011/07/15/the-first-12-dow-components-where-are-they-now/ for further details.

(4) GPFG's approach does not naturally complement national balance sheet. It is using oil revenues to invest in many large market capitalization companies that are oil producers. Most notably, NBIM has excluded resource company Rio Tinto Group from its investment universe due to environmental issues.

(5) Finally, there are some concerns that Norway's overly transparent disclosure may pass on information that may move the market (given GPFG's size), ultimately hurting its performance. For instance, any changes in risk premia views may be seen by the market as a sell signal on a specific country or sector, encouraging other market participants to liquidate ahead of GPFG.

2.3.2 *Risk Analysis Example — Temasek Holdings*

In this subsection, we analyze the performance of Temasek Holdings. The performance graph shown in Figure 2.4 is taken from information made public by Temasek Holdings on its 2010 Annual Report[15].

Temasek is known to have a set of internal allocation targets based on a combination of 40% in Asia ex-Japan and ex-Singapore, 30% in Singapore, 20% in OECD Economies, as well as 10% in Rest of World, with a focus primarily on Latin America and Africa. Based on these internal targets, we use a basket of liquid-market proxies as shown in Table 2.1 to construct a benchmark performance time series. Latin America and Africa are considered to be primarily a resource "play", thus we feel that the most appropriate liquid-market proxy in such a case will be the Goldman Sachs Commodity Index (GSCI). In addition, we further optimize the asset allocation of the composite benchmarks using a commercial optimizer, based on the two schemes as described in Lee (2006) and Lee, Rogal and Weinberger (2010), under ranges of 0% to 40%. These approaches are consistent with the typical asset allocation methodologies used by long-term investors to manage real-life multi-asset portfolios. The resulting optimized allocations, as shown in Table 2.2, are found to show superior return-to-drawdown characteristics. Figure 2.5 is constructed to further compare the performance based on the balance sheet values of Temasek (published on its Annual Report) to these synthetic benchmarks. We believe that balance sheet values will give a reasonably accurate picture of Temasek's net asset values (NAV) in a manner consistent with typical NAV reporting done by any commercial institutional asset manager such as a hedge fund. All performance figures are scaled to 100 at the end of March, 2005, which coincides with the fiscal year end of Temasek Holdings.

---

[15] Available from http://www.temasekreport.com/2010/documents/full_annual_report2010.pdf.

Some interesting observations from Figure 2.5 include:

(1) *Prior to 2008* — There is almost no observable alpha in Temasek's portfolio before the dramatic events of 2008.

(2) *Gains in 2008* — Since our analysis is done based on a straightforward currency translation without any currency hedging, and Temasek's portfolio is likely to have some degree of currency hedging, the gains in 2008 may be partially due to Temasek gaining from currency hedging after the significant strengthening of the Singapore dollar.

(3) *Drawdown in 2009* — Notice that Temasek's drawdown is significantly milder than its synthetic benchmarks based on liquid-market proxies. However, a meaningful portion of Temasek's portfolio is private, and Temasek's fiscal-year-end results were not released until August of 2009, by which time the markets had experienced a meaningful recovery. It is certainly not unheard of for privately-held investments to report retroactive valuations to reflect improved market sentiments, although such practice may not necessarily be reflected in this case. We are simply posing a fair question based on common market practice.

(4) *Rebounds in 2010* — Notice how the public markets did not recover its full losses from the end of March in 2008 to the end of March in 2010, while Temasek did. It will be interesting to attribute the superior performance of Temasek in terms of: i) currency gains, ii) any possible "cushioning" in valuations by privately-held investments, or iii) superior alpha selection.

Table 2.1   Temasek Holdings' Internal Benchmarks

Geographical Region	Internal Target	2010 Allocation	Liquid Market Proxy
Asia ex-Japan and ex-Singapore	40%	46%	MSCI Asia ex-Japan
Singapore	30%	32%	Straits Times Index
OECD Economies	20%	20%	S&P500 Index
Others	10%	2%	GS Commodity Index

Table 2.2   Temasek Holdings' Internal Benchmarks and Optimized Allocations

Liquid Market Proxy	Internal Target	Sharpe-Ratio Optimized	Alternative Sharpe-Ratio Optimized
MSCI Asia ex-Japan	40%	40%	33%
Straits Times Index	30%	40%	40%
S&P500 Index	20%	0%	0%
GS Commodity Index	10%	20%	27%

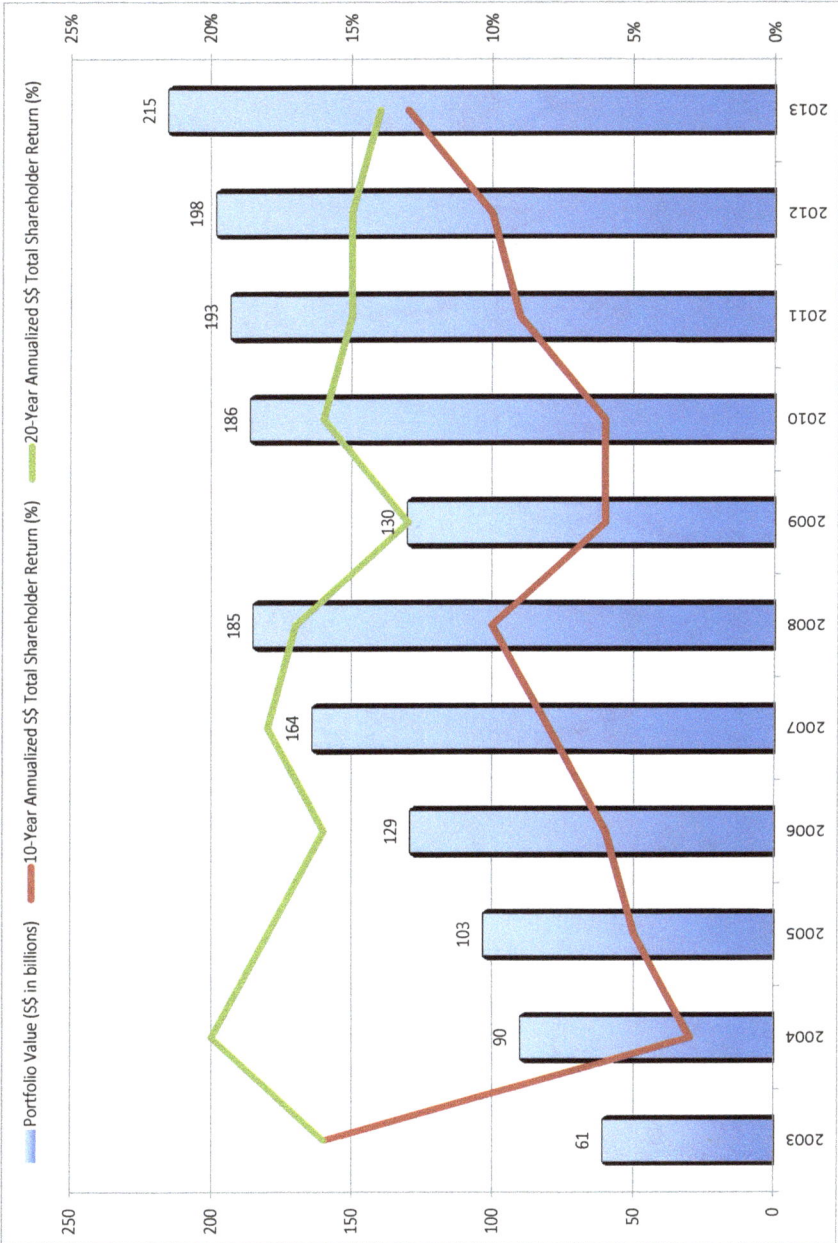

Fig. 2.4 Temasek's Portfolio Value in Singapore Dollars Published by Temasek Holdings' 2012 and 2013 Annual Reports

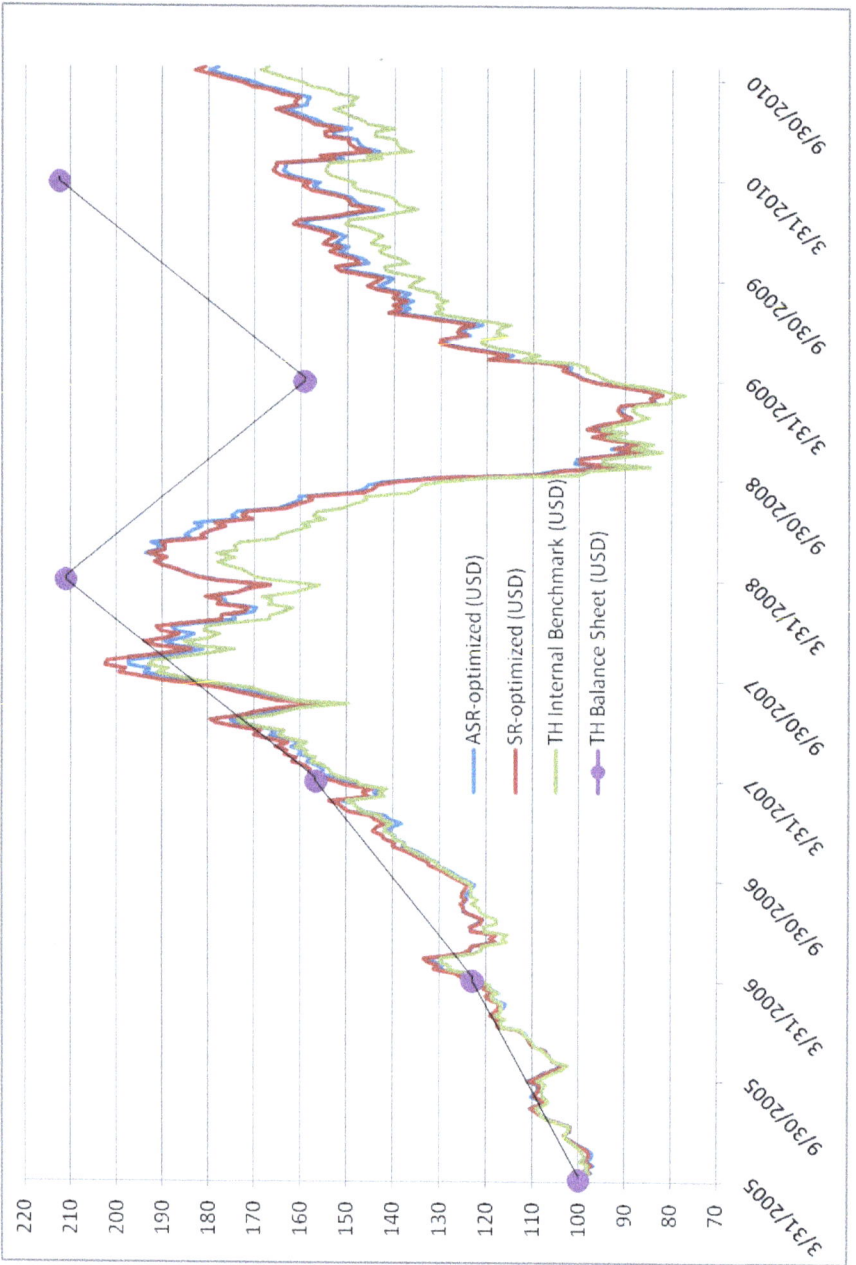

Fig. 2.5 Temasek Holdings' Balance Sheet Values Relative to Synthetic Benchmarks (in US dollars, assuming no currency hedging)

In light of the facts and analysis above, it seems puzzling that with all the comparative advantages of SWFs over other investors in the market, there is no significant evidence that SWFs can deliver persistent long-term over-performance. Although there are potential drawbacks to each of the distinctive features of these government-owned funds, we feel that one plausible explanation may lie in not having the right set of performance measures to evaluate the unique nature and purpose of SWF investments.

SWFs are set up to serve their countries by preserving wealth across multiple generations of its people. Compared to commercially-delegated investment institutions, whose only purpose is to seek the highest-available financial returns for their investors, a SWF generally has to face a slightly different set of political agenda that creates strategic benefits to a national economy. These investments by all means serve the fund's investors — the people of its sponsoring country — however, the financial profits that come along with these strategic benefits may not be apparent in a short-term horizon, over which most of the existing performance evaluation methodologies are applied. While the potential long-run financial benefits of these strategic investments are hard to measure, at the minimum any short-term performance measures should not penalize SWFs for meeting those longer-term strategic objectives. In particular, the long-horizon nature of SWF investments should be taken into special consideration during the fund managers' performance evaluation. Otherwise, the finite tenure of fund managers and endowment sponsors will only encourage significant short-term risk-aversion behavior, which may erode the strategic benefits of being able to invest over longer-term horizons. Such problems should be properly addressed in finding suitable performance evaluation measures for fund managers responsible for SWF investments.

From a pure financial economics perspective, the massive size of SWF investments creates another challenge for performance evaluation of "active" management. "Active" management can be measured by the difference between the return on a fund and the returns on its benchmark portfolio. If the fund manager passively invests according to the benchmark, the "active return" of the fund would be zero. Traditional performance measures are benchmarked against the market of liquid securities. During the 2008 financial crisis, these systematic factors, which explain a significant component of performance, performed quite poorly. In addition, the massive size of SWF investments may have large price impact on these benchmark measures.

For these reasons, the author proposes the following set of principles to construct a fair performance benchmark for SWFs:

(1) discourage SWFs from simply piling into equities or any other "vogue" investments;

(2) encourage "alpha" investments that can promote national economic development;

(3) encourage investments in sectors complementary to national balance sheets to create natural diversification effects;

(4) disallow domination by certain countries with massive public reserves (e.g. the PRC), so that countries with smaller public reserves may feel that such a benchmark will be entirely irrelevant to their needs; and

(5) be based on reasonably liquid assets with regular mark-to-market values.

One possible approach is to create a peer benchmark by value-weighing the asset allocations of all major SWFs. SWFs smaller than say US$100 billion in net asset values will be rescaled to US$100 billion to ensure that they will be given a meaningful minimum weight. In each asset class, a fixed number (e.g. 100) of "investable" assets that are most heavily invested by SWFs will be selected to represent the performance of that asset class. Doing so will construct a peer performance index that satisfies most if not all of the characteristics as stated above.

Beyond a peer benchmark, how does a typical SWF access investments at the asset level or at the different portfolio management team level? Such assessment is important for the sponsor to assess whether the respective portfolio management team should take active risk, how much they are expected to deliver for each asset.

As an example, based on a mock portfolio of Temasek's publicly available positions, we have calculated the implied returns of its position in American International Group (AIG) to be 12.46% versus a one-year return of 37.16%. On a one-year basis, AIG has generated close to 25% of out-performance relative to its break-even return. That, however, does not imply that AIG is a compelling investment proposition over the medium term, or the type of investment horizons that truly matter to sovereign wealth funds. For comparison, we then created a medium term economic scenario based on views from an "Uncertain Middle Road" scenario on US employment discussed by Dr. Mohamed El-Erian, Chief Executive Officer of PIMCO[16]. Based on a regression model using standard factors including the S&P 500 index, US Treasury 10-year yield, euro-US dollar exchange rate and gold prices, AIG is expected to return 1.27%, but its implied return under such a scenario is 0.1%. In other words, while there will be medium term out-performance, any out-performance will be considerably more modest than what is observable based on a one-year period.

---

[16]Excerpted from http://www.bloomberg.com/video/pimco-s-el-erian-on-april-u-s-jobs-data-fMIyQrkpSi-75pXnEBAw4w.html.

This type of calculations can be aggregated so that it can be done for each asset class or even for a mix of asset classes (in the case of hybrid assets such as infrastructure where "charging rates" can be based on a mix of bond and equity). In addition, for more senior portfolio managers with responsibility for allocating capital across different teams, there is a consistent way to measure the success of his allocation relative to what one may describe as a "policy" benchmark.

2.3.3 *Practical Allocation Between Active and Passive Portfolios*

Imagine a hypothetical country looking to invest a trillion dollars in excess reserves. It seeks a balanced approach to asset allocation. These reserves are not purely resource-driven, so its national balance sheet profile matters instead of taking a pure non-commodity passive approach similar to that adopted by Norway. Perhaps one pragmatic allocation solution is to blend the passive approach taken by the Norwegians with the private-equity-like approach taken by Temasek. The private equity allocation can be used to complement the national balance sheet while the passive component ensures that its people receives cost-efficient market returns.

Based on the latest AUM figures reported in 2013, the Norwegian portfolio is worth US$717 billion, with roughly a 60-40 split between equity and bond, while the Temasek portfolio is worth US$173 billion. Thus, we can simply create an aggregated portfolio of US$890 billion based on the combined assets held — as such there is factual proof that the size is investable, as follows:

Table 2.3   Composite of Norwegian GPFG and Temasek Portfolios

Allocation	Passive Bond	Passive Equity	Active Equity
Weights	32%	48%	20%
One-Year Historical Returns (Aug 2012 to Aug 2013)	4.32%	16.67%	4.69%
Implied Returns	5.25%	12.76%	11.53%

Table 2.3 suggests that, while the bond allocation of this composite portfolio is roughly generating the returns that it is expected to generate, Active Equity is under-performing while Passive Equity is out-performing. A rational asset allocator will reduce allocation to Active Equity while increasing allocation to Passive Equity. Interestingly enough, the implied return for its entire Equity bucket of 12.40% is roughly comparable to its historical return of 12.98%, suggesting that the issue is about the sub-allocation between Active Equity and Passive Equity.

The example above is based on one-year return. The "private equity"-like holdings of Temasek should be viewed from the perspective of a typical holding horizon of 5 to 10 years. This analysis can simply be repeated using a medium-term economic view. The asset allocator can then work out the most appropriate allocation to Passive Bond, Passive Equity and Active Equity in such a portfolio for the medium term.

2.4 Summary

This chapter studies about how global asset management reaches its current state of domination by SWFs, by discussing the following:

(1) historical development;
(2) key players and investment approaches; and
(3) investment risk and performance characteristics.

The key trends observed include:

(1) From a few specialized, marginal players, SWFs are transforming into a dominating force in institutional asset management;
(2) From active managers primarily managing wealth in an endowment format, SWFs are increasingly recognizing that their size makes it most difficult to achieve spectacular active returns and they allocate assets accordingly; and
(3) From mimicking large commercial managers, SWFs are beginning to develop their own approach to asset management given their unique roles in the global economy.

These observations lead to the natural next step to answer deeper questions on how to best address the asset management needs of SWFs as seen today.

Chapter 3

Evolving Roles

3.1 Introduction

This chapter presents a parsimonious model that is roughly consistent with the current state of the global economy. Such a model can be used to better understand possible policy options and the evolving roles of SWFs in today's turbulent global financial markets.

3.1.1 *Motivation*

In 2006, the author proposed a SWF asset allocation model that uses the following portfolio objective function that incorporates fourth-order statistics in Lee (2006):

$$ASR \equiv \frac{\sum_i e_i \pi_i}{z_\pi^- \sigma_\pi} + \frac{1}{2} \frac{\sum_i \pi_i \left(z_i^+ \sigma_i\right)^2}{z_\pi^- \sigma_\pi} - \frac{1}{2} z_\pi^- \sigma_\pi \tag{3.1}$$

where:

e_i is expected return of the i-th asset,

π_i is portfolio weight of the i-th asset,

σ_i and σ_π are volatilities of the i-th asset and of the portfolio, respectively,

$z_i^+ = \frac{max\left(z_{cf}\left(z_C^+(i)\right),0\right)}{z_C^+}$ where z_C^+ is "upside" critical value for probability α,

$z_\pi^- = \frac{min\left(z_{cf}\left(z_C^-(\pi)\right),0\right)}{z_C^-}$ where z_C^- is "downside" critical value for probability $1 - \alpha$,

and

z_{cf} is the fourth-order Cornish-Fisher coefficient that corresponds to the fat-tail adjustment for the asset return distribution (with S and K denoting observed skewness and kurtosis statistics), i.e.:

$$z_{cf} = z_C + \frac{1}{6}\left(z_C^2 - 1\right)S + \frac{1}{24}\left(z_C^3 - 3z_C\right)K + \frac{1}{36}\left(2z_C^3 - 5z_C\right)S^2$$

This performance metric, called the Alternative Sharpe Ratio in Lee & Lee (2004a), has properties similar to those of the "Omega function" proposed by Keating & Shadwick (2005) and other loss functions used in actuarial mathematics. It can be shown that the metric provides a number of mathematical properties helpful to portfolio managers:

(1) If a particular asset in the portfolio shows positive skewness (or "upside" characteristics), this portfolio performance metric will improve;

(2) If a particular asset in the portfolio contributes to "downside" portfolio tail risk, this portfolio performance metric will be penalized; and

(3) If all assets in the portfolio have normally as well as independently and identically distributed returns, this portfolio performance metric will revert to the typical second-order portfolio performance metric of the Sharpe Ratio.

When applied with proper caution, this type of sophisticated asset allocation technique can make the appropriate adjustments to account for tail-risk behavior in asset returns. In contrast, traditional asset allocation techniques are mostly based on second-order objective functions, which are known to be biased in favor of high-tail-risk strategies such as "short put options" without capturing their risk of catastrophic losses. Empirically, second-order techniques tend to generate abruptly different allocations after each realization of a tail-risk event. Given the massive size of a typical SWF, it will be at best problematic for such mega-sized asset allocator to apply standard second-order asset allocation techniques in practical portfolio management, because SWFs cannot easily liquidate, rebalance, or hedge out undesirable risk factor exposures at will. The defining limitation faced by a rational SWF asset allocator is that any major allocation decision, once executed, may not be easily reversible; therefore, a rational allocator needs to price in "once-in-a-decade" tail events ahead of implementing any portfolio decision. This proposed technique has been presented in publications linked to the World Bank [Lee (2006)], the European Central Bank and the Bank for International Settlement [Lee, Rogal & Weinberger (2010)], and most recently the Asian Development Bank [Lee & Wang (2011)].

With that background, the author now moves beyond stand-alone asset allocation models computed from the perspective of a single allocator. Typical asset allocation models *assume* the abundance of liquidity, in that it is feasible for the allocation decision to be executed without moving the markets significantly. The unique challenges faced by SWFs are that: (1) Their fund size may approach that of one or more liquid markets; in fact, there is at least one case that a SWF comes quite close to dominating the entire market (Table 3.1 illustrates the impressive number of component stocks in the Straits Times Index held by Temasek Holdings); and (2) Such a fund may become the primary source of available market liquidity in a crisis scenario, making it infeasible for them to execute any reallocation after the eruption of a crisis. The reality is that some of these SWFs have grown sufficiently big that any major asset rebalancing even under normal market conditions will almost certainly cause significant market movements. A "good" allocation decision may turn "bad" if the very act of making the allocation can drive up the target asset price by a large amount, or one such decision may compel another mega-sized investor to respond in such a way that accentuates further market instability.

The explicit goal of this chapter is to eliminate the "smoke and mirrors" of complex mathematics typically found among sophisticated asset allocation models in order to better understand the underlying issues using a relatively parsimonious approach. In particular, we have deliberately avoided superimposing any asset allocation model with complex market-impact dynamics, which may be necessary in order to give an explicit description of the asset rebalancing process by an investor comparable in size to a SWF. Doing so may result in a model with way too many degrees of freedom to be helpful. To the best of the author's knowledge, most SWFs stay away from highly complex quantitative asset allocation models, partly because the incorporation and calibration of market impact models are far from satisfactory for typical transactions running in the billions of dollars. One goal in this exercise is to demonstrate that it is possible to construct an intellectually sound yet compact model, which can also produce practical recommendations that are appealing to the Chief Investment Officers of SWFs.

3.1.2 *Recap on the Lee (2006) Approach*

Research in optimal portfolio strategies by Merton (1998) describes how long-term wealth managers should consider not only contemporaneous asset holdings, but also the potential substitution effects due to anticipated inflow and outflow characteristics. Lee (2006) further expanded on the basic model of Merton to better understand asset allocation from a national balance sheet perspective, assuming that the global economy is populated by three types of countries, as already shown in Figure 1.1 in Chapter 1:

(1) Group A — Countries in Group A have abundant natural resources;
(2) Group B — Countries in Group B have abundant productive labor and favor the production of manufactured goods; and
(3) Group C — Countries in Group C have abundant intangible assets, such as in-

Table 3.1   Components of the Straits Times Index (*Not*) Held by Temasek Holdings

Rank	Constituent Name	Subsector Name	Weight in Index (%)
1	Singapore Telecom	Telecommunications	9.78
2	DBS Group Holdings	Banks	9.59
3	*Overseas-Chinese Banking*	*Banks*	*8.47*
4	*United Overseas Bank*	*Banks*	*8.44*
5	Wilmar International Limited	Food Products	6.76
6	Capitaland	Development	4.88
7	*Jardine Matheson*	*Diversified Industrials*	*4.64*
8	*Hong Kong Land*	*Development*	*4.55*
9	Keppel Corp	Diversified Industrials	4.10
10	Noble Group	Diversified Industrials	3.76
11	Singapore Airlines	Airlines	3.68
12	Singapore Exchange	Investment Services	3.30
13	City Development	Hotels	2.80
14	Fraser and Neave	Diversified Industrials	2.45
15	Singapore Press Holdings	Publishing	2.37
16	*Jardine Strategic*	*Diversified Industrials*	*2.36*
17	Golden Agri-Resources	Airlines	2.02
18	Singapore Tech. Engineering	Aerospace	1.88
19	Genting Singapore	Recreational Services	1.77
20	CapitalMall Trust	Retail REITs	1.71
21	*Jardine Cycle & Carriage*	*Specialty Retailers*	*1.52*
22	Olam International	Food Products	1.51
23	CapitalMall Asia	Development	1.44
24	SembCorp Industries	Diversified Industrials	1.38
25	SembCorp Marine	Transportation Services	1.30
26	ComfortDelgro Corp	Travel & Tourism	1.27
27	Neptune Orient Lines	Marine Transportation	0.79
28	StarHub	Telecommunications	0.59
29	SMRT Corp	Travel & Tourism	0.59
30	SIA Engineering	Transportation Services	0.31
Total			**100**

Holdings of Temasek as of April 2011. Components of the Straits Times Index have since been replaced, but our assessment remains unchanged. Companies not held by Temasek are listed in **bold-italics**.

tellectual property, scientific and technical leadership, high-value-added managerial skills, capital market expertise including stock markets, hedge funds and venture capital investments.

Lee (2006) has assumed that one dominant country in Group C issues the major trade settlement currency in this global economy. The author was able to demonstrate by computing asset allocations using empirical market data how each of these Groups will follow these asset allocation policy responses:

(1) Group A — These resource-rich countries are naturally "long" resources and "long" the global trade settlement currency (as a result of selling their natural resources). Their appropriate diversification policy is to sell resources forward and invest their global trade settlement currency reserves by buying manufacturing goods and intangible assets.

(2) Group B — These manufacturing powerhouses are naturally "short" resources and "long" the global trade settlement currency (as a result of producing and selling their manufacturing goods). Their appropriate diversification policy is to buy resources as well as intangible assets.

(3) Group C — The primary "exports" of these countries are intangible assets, such as equity and debt papers. Their appropriate diversification policy is to develop more value-added services (and hence intangible assets) related to resources and manufacturing. An example could be to develop an advanced oil/gas services sector and expertise in managing the complex logistics of global manufacturing.

Table 3.2 shows one optimal allocation calculated for Groups A and B based on empirical market data, under the initial assumptions that Group A is significantly "long" crude oil while Group B is significantly "short" crude oil. In fact, depending on the commodity index being used, it can be shown that Group A should sell resources forward while Group B should stockpile resources to meet its expected demands.

Table 3.2 Optimized Allocations for Groups A and B

Asset Class	Group A	Group B
*Crude Oil**	*50%*	*-25%*
Commodity Index	5%	5%
Cash Equivalent	25%	100%
Equity	20%	20%
Balance Sheet Total	**100%**	**100%**

* Based on the initial assumptions (from Lee (2006)) that Group A is "long" crude oil while Group B is "short" crude oil.

What is still missing from the analysis above is the potential impact of immigration and knowledge transfer — specifically, the flow of skills and expertise from Group C countries to Group A and B countries, making the distinctions among Groups A, B and C increasingly blurred. A natural outcome of this model is that there will be Group A and Group B countries accumulating large public surpluses to invest in debt and equity papers issued by Group C countries. The picture portrayed above works well until one of the following boundary conditions is reached: (1) Certain Group A countries start running low in natural resources; or (2) Certain Group C countries start running into a crisis of market confidence. Group B countries are in a slightly more enviable position because manufacturing can be retooled (despite the potential costs involved), and there will always be some demands for certain manufacturing goods. By comparison, corrective actions may not be available when natural resources are depleted, or when the market no longer has confidence to support the high valuation of intangible assets created by a certain country.

There is one significant shortcoming in the techniques discussed so far. In the absence of practical market constraints, any optimal asset allocation computed purely from empirical market data will recommend essentially the same optimum for all countries, with the primary difference given by pre-existing long or short positions from national balance sheets prior to netting. However, constraints matter for mega-sized investors at the global level. The most obvious example is that there is only a finite amount of crude oil available globally even after counting unextracted reserves, so it may be infeasible for all Groups to allocate to crude oil simultaneously. In that case, deriving any such asset allocation using existing market prices will be misleading, because they do not reflect executable prices that a SWF may likely transact on, unless a "market impact" function is constructed for the scenario in which all SWFs are buying crude oil simultaneously. Similarly, Group C cannot issue significantly more new securities without the corresponding interest by Groups A and B to make allocations to such securities. A meaningful SWF asset allocation model must incorporate such relationships into its mathematical formulation, instead of solving the SWF allocation problem as an abstract stand-alone problem from the perspective of a single allocator.

In this chapter, we will move beyond stand-alone asset allocation models computed from the perspective of a single allocator by observing that any mathematical allocation solutions, however sophisticated, are often rendered infeasible by the unique global market constraints faced by mega-sized investors, and that such constraints instead of the objective function end up driving the solution. Therefore, we focus on what matters the most by building a model of aggregated flows and constraints on the global economy faced by a SWF asset allocator. Once the feasible set is defined, we will then explore the applicability of the appropriate allocation models.

3.1.3 *Roadmap*

In the remainder of this chapter, Section 3.2 provides a mathematical description of our global economy based on the consequences of the SWF asset allocation process as described in Lee (2006). Section 3.3 will seek to better understand the potential outcomes of policy interventions in such a global economy. Section 3.4 will make an attempt to understand the implications of our model to SWF investing. Section 3.5 summarizes.

3.2   Abstract Model of Global Economy

To simplify the modeling approach used in Lee (2006), there are now only 3 countries (instead of 3 groups of countries) in our formulation of the global economy:

(1) *Country A* — Rich in resources;
(2) *Country B* — Rich in productive labor; and
(3) *Country C* — Imports resources and manufactured goods and exports innovation and intellectual capital.

Most asset allocation decisions made by a typical SWF tend to be relatively static, because of its size relative to liquid markets and therefore the time required to change holdings without moving the markets. The goal of this section is to provide a parsimonious description of the aggregated flows among countries and reasonable constraints within the global economy. There are a number of large-scale econometric models in existence (e.g. Oxford Economics) that explicitly provide such descriptions using published macroeconomic statistics. Those models often involve at least a few hundred equations and perhaps even more variables. Given the high degrees of freedom involved, there may be considerable challenges in extracting useful insights by using any such model to solve an asset allocation problem.

3.2.1 *Basic Descriptions*

General Assumptions:

All countries start with the same level of initial endowment as a boundary condition. This may be seen as a bold assumption, but it is not inappropriate as the focus of our analysis is the steady-state behavior of allocation decisions. If national wealth is evidently drained from one country to another at steady state, it is easier to understand the steady-state behavior when all countries start at equal levels. Consistent with Lee (2006), Country C is the issuer of the single global trade settlement currency, and the only issuer of public debts and public equities. We specify the following for each country:

(1) *Net Asset Value on National Balance Sheet* — Net Asset Value (NAV) will be computed from an asset management accounting perspective, in that we are only counting *tangible* assets.

(2) *Cash* — Our current assumption is that there is a single global trade settlement currency. We also assume that only short-term bonds with a constant short-term rate are issued and they are considered cash equivalent. We note that there is an active debate on whether bonds should be considered close substitutes of cash after the 2008 financial crisis. We are adopting a simple modeling choice to avoid any need for a term structure of interest rate that will create significant complications on deriving dividend discount rates and equity valuation.

(3) *Investments* — Portions of reserves managed by SWFs (i.e. cash and investments make up a surplus country's total reserves). We note that, in at least two countries, reserves in cash and bonds are managed by the central bank, while various other forms of equity holdings (public versus private, domestic versus foreign) are managed via different vehicles. For the purpose of understanding the appropriate investment choices to be made by a public surplus manager, we do not believe any significant insights will be gained by the holding structure of investment vehicles in finer details.

(4) *Commodities* — We assume that this represents primarily metals and other mineral wealth, since soft commodities typically represent minor portions of the total wealth in countries of interest to this analysis. From a national balance sheet perspective, both extracted as well as unextracted mineral reserves should be counted.

(5) *Basic Trade Flows* — In a closed global economy, the sum total of all net imports and net exports should be zero.

(6) *Equity and Debts "Issued"* — Issuance is listed on the liability column of the national balance sheet. The values of Equity and Debts are functions of factors such as price, holdings and dividend discount rates. However, we do not see any need to create any complex mathematical specification at this stage, except to point out that Equity has no theoretical limits on its value while the principal on Debts can at best be valued at par. Notice that Equity here only denotes equity *issued* and publicly sold. As one may expect, there will be equity values on state balance sheets such as infrastructure or state land

that are neither issued as equity nor sold to the public. Such equity values are not counted as part of equity *issued* for the purpose of this discussion.

(7) *Proxy Price Index* — The Proxy Price Index or PPI is defined as $PPI(t) = \frac{Cash+Investment}{Commodity}$, i.e. the aggregate amount of cash and investments available relative to each unit of physical Commodity within a domestic economy. Notice that domestic prices of Commodities can be different from country to country, even though the same Commodity can be priced in different countries dominated in a single global trade settlement currency; in real-life commodity trading, that is also known as "delivery spread". The proposed representation is consistent with the concept of asset inflation: If a country is "printing money" or it is experiencing an investment bull market, it may suffer from inflation since the commodity base is somewhat static in general. Such a ratio will then increase, as is consistent with real-world observations. Our initial assumption is that Country A enjoys a lower Proxy Price Index initially because it is endowed with more abundant resources, while Countries B and C will have the same purchasing power initially — by giving Countries B and C equal purchasing power initially, it is easier to observe the expected behavior of the model as it approaches steady state.

3.2.2 *Country A — Rich in Resources*

The asset and liability profiles of Country A can be described as follows:

$$Asset_A(t) = Cash_A(t) + Commodity_A(t) + Investment_A(t) \qquad (3.2)$$

$$Liability_A(t) = Equity_A(t) + Debt_A(t) + NetAsset_A(t) \qquad (3.3)$$

We assume that Country A does not need to issue debts and equities. Equations (3.2) and (3.3) above imply that Country A will start out as a net creditor, as in:

$$NetAsset_A(t) = Cash_A(t) + Commodity_A(t) + Investment_A(t) \qquad (3.4)$$

Notice that $NetAsset_A$ appears on the liability side of the equation as it represents a claim on Country A's wealth by its citizens. This is expressed in standard net asset value representation used in asset management, in that we are only counting *tangible* accounting items.

The following initial conditions and temporal change relationships are roughly consistent with the findings of Lee (2006), but the numbers have been rounded off to simple units for the ease of analysis. We do not believe that any significant insights will be gained by calibrating these numbers to those of specific countries, but doing so may needlessly complicate our modeling efforts:

Initial Conditions:

$$Asset_A\,(0) = 100$$

$$Cash_A\,(0) = 25$$

$$Commodity_A\,(0) = 50$$

$$Investment_A\,(0) = 25$$

$$PPI_A\,(0) = \frac{25 + 25}{50} = 1$$

Temporal Changes:

$$NetExport_A\,(t) = -2.5$$

Negative sign means net imports because it represents a payment.

$$Commodity_A\,(t) - Commodity_A\,(t + 1) = 5$$

The positive sign represents the annual sales of commodity as a result of commodities production. Since the asset equation should balance, any net sales in commodity will translate into receipts in cash and investment.

$$Asset_A\,(t + 1) = Asset_A\,(t) + NetExport_A(t)$$

The relationship above assumes a single-period delay for the payment of account payables.

Net Asset Value:

$$Cash_A\,(t + 1) + Commodity_A\,(t + 1) + Investment_A\,(t + 1) =$$
$$Cash_A\,(t) + Commodity_A\,(t) + Investment_A\,(t) + NetExport_A\,(t) \quad (3.5)$$

Equation (3.5) assumes that cash and investments do not change valuation and their proportional allocation remains static. This assumption will be revisited in Section 3.4. From Equation (3.5), we have:

$$Cash_A\,(t + 1) + Investment_A\,(t + 1) =$$
$$Cash_A\,(t) + Investment_A\,(t) + NetExport_A\,(t)$$
$$+ Commodity_A\,(t) - Commodity_A\,(t + 1) \quad (3.6)$$

Simplifying based on the temporal change relationships as stated above,

$$Cash_A\,(t + 1) + Investment_A\,(t + 1) = Cash_A\,(t) + Investment_A\,(t) + 2.5 \quad (3.7)$$

3.2.3 *Country B — Rich in Labor*

The asset and liability profiles of Country B can be described as follows:

$$Asset_B(t) = Cash_B(t) + Commodity_B(t) + Investment_B(t) \qquad (3.8)$$

$$Liability_B(t) = Equity_B(t) + Debt_B(t) + NetAsset_B(t) \qquad (3.9)$$

Likewise, we assume that Country B does not need to issue debts and equities. Equations (3.8) and (3.9) imply that Country B will start out as a net creditor, as in:

$$NetAsset_B(t) = Cash_B(t) + Commodity_B(t) + Investment_B(t) \qquad (3.10)$$

Notice that $NetAsset_B$ appears on the liability side of the equation as it represents a claim on Country B's wealth by its citizens. This is expressed in standard net asset value representation used in asset management, in that we are only counting *tangible* accounting items.

The following initial conditions and temporal change relationships are roughly consistent with the findings of Lee (2006), but the numbers have been rounded off to simple units for the ease of analysis. We do not believe that any significant insights will be gained by calibrating these numbers to those of specific countries, but doing so may needlessly complicate our modeling efforts:

Initial Conditions:

$$Asset_B(0) = 100$$

$$Cash_B(0) = 50$$

$$Commodity_B(0) = 25$$

$$Investment_B(0) = 25$$

$$PPI_B(0) = \frac{50 + 25}{25} = 3$$

Temporal Changes:

$$NetExport_B(t) = 5$$

Positive sign means net receipts from exports.

$$Commodity_B(t) - Commodity_B(t + 1) = -2.5$$

Negative sign represents the annual purchase of commodity as a result of the consumption of commodities. Since the asset equation should balance, any net purchase in commodity will translate into payments in cash and investment.

$$Asset_B (t + 1) = Asset_B (t) + NetExport_B(t)$$

The relationship above assumes a single-period delay for the collection of account receivables.

<u>Net Asset Value:</u>

$$Cash_B (t + 1) + Commodity_B (t + 1) + Investment_B (t + 1) =$$

$$Cash_B (t) + Commodity_B (t) + Investment_B (t) + NetExport_B (t) \quad (3.11)$$

Equation (3.11) assumes that cash and investments do not change valuation and their proportional allocation remains static. This assumption will be revisited in Section 3.4. From Equation (3.11), we have:

$$Cash_B (t + 1) + Investment_B (t + 1) =$$

$$Cash_B (t) + Investment_B (t) + NetExport_B (t)$$

$$+ Commodity_B (t) - Commodity_B (t + 1) \quad (3.12)$$

Simplifying based on the temporal change relationships as stated above,

$$Cash_B (t + 1) + Investment_B (t + 1) = Cash_B (t) + Investment_B (t) + 2.5 \quad (3.13)$$

3.2.4   *Country C — Rich in Intellectual Properties/Innovation*

The asset and liability profiles of Country C can be described as follows:

$$Asset_C (t) = Cash_C (t) + Commodity_C (t) + Investment_C (t) \quad (3.14)$$

$$Liability_C (t) = Equity_C (t) + Debt_C (t) + NetAsset_C (t) \quad (3.15)$$

Notice that *NetAsset_C* appears on the liability column as it represents a claim on Country C's wealth by its citizens. This is expressed in standard net asset value representation used in asset management, in that we are only counting *tangible* accounting items.

The following initial conditions and temporal change relationships are constructed so that Country C will issue 100 units each of Equity and Debt to be held by all countries in the global economy. The initial conditions have been rounded off to simple units for the ease of analysis. We do not believe that any significant insights will be gained by calibrating these numbers to those of specific countries, but doing so may needlessly complicate our modeling efforts:

$$Equity_C(0) = 100$$

$$Debt_C(0) = 100$$

Initial Conditions:

$$Asset_C(0) = 100$$

$$Cash_C(0) = 25$$

$$Commodity_C(0) = 25$$

$$Investment_C(0) = 50$$

$$PPI_C(0) = \frac{25 + 50}{25} = 3$$

Based on these initial conditions, Country C will issue more debts and equities than it has *tangible* assets. Therefore, Country C will start out in a negative net asset position:

$$NetAsset_C(t) = Cash_C(t) + Commodity_C(t) + Investment_C(t)$$
$$- Equity_C(t) - Debt_C(t)$$

In real-world accounting, it is not uncommon for entities such as pre-revenue high-tech companies to issue more debts and equities than it has *tangible* assets, but one can expect intangible accounting items such as goodwill or book value of intellectual property to be recorded on the asset column of its balance sheet. In such cases, those items will be counted as part of $NetAsset_C(t)$.

Temporal Changes:

$$NetExport_C(t) = -(NetExport_A(t) + NetExport_B(t)) = -2.5$$

In other words, the sum of net exports from all countries must be zero since global net imports and exports should balance.

$$Commodity_C(t) - Commodity_C(t+1) = -2.5$$

Negative sign represents the annual purchase of commodity as a result of the consumption of commodities. Since the asset equation must balance, net purchases in commodity will translate into payments in cash and investment.

$$Asset_C (t + 1) = Asset_C (t) + NetExport_C(t)$$

The relationship above assumes a single-period delay for the payment of account payables.

Moreover, a closed global economy must observe the following additional temporal change relationships:

$$Equity_C (t) = Investment_A (t) + Investment_B (t) + Investment_C (t) \qquad (3.16)$$

Equation (3.16) assumes that Country C creates the world's only equity issues available.

$$Debt_C (t) = Cash_A (t) + Cash_B (t) + Cash_C (t) \qquad (3.17)$$

Equation (3.17) assumes that Country C creates the world's currency and cash equivalent, i.e. the world's trading currency is in fact short-term obligations of Country C.

Net Asset Value:

$$Cash_C (t + 1) + Commodity_C (t + 1) + Investment_C (t + 1)$$
$$- Debt_C (t + 1) - Equity_C (t + 1) =$$
$$Cash_C (t) + Commodity_C (t) + Investment_C (t)$$
$$- Debt_C (t) - Equity_C (t) + NetExport_C (t) \qquad (3.18)$$

Equation (3.18) assumes cash and investments do not change valuation and their proportional allocation remains static. This assumption will be revisited in Section 3.4. From Equation (3.18), we have:

$$Cash_C (t + 1) + Investment_C (t + 1) - Debt_C (t + 1) - Equity_C (t + 1) =$$
$$Cash_C (t) + Investment_C (t) - Debt_C(t) - Equity_C(t)$$
$$+ Commodity_C (t) - Commodity_C (t + 1) + NetExport_C (t) \qquad (3.19)$$

Simplifying based on the temporal change relationships as stated above,

$$Cash_C (t + 1) + Investment_C (t + 1) - Debt_C (t + 1) - Equity_C (t + 1) =$$
$$Cash_C (t) + Investment_C (t) - Debt_C (t) - Equity_C (t) - 5 \qquad (3.20)$$

3.2.5 *Analysis in the Absence of Policy Actions*

We will analyze the implications from the following representation of the global economy as a system of difference equations (3.7), (3.13) and (3.20):

$$Cash_A (t + 1) + Investment_A (t + 1) = Cash_A (t) + Investment_A (t) + 2.5$$

$$Cash_B (t + 1) + Investment_B (t + 1) = Cash_B (t) + Investment_B (t) + 2.5$$

$$Cash_C (t + 1) + Investment_C (t + 1) - Debt_C (t + 1) - Equity_C (t + 1) =$$
$$Cash_C (t) + Investment_C (t) - Debt_C (t) - Equity_C (t) - 5$$

In this system, Country C issues debts and equities in order to finance its imports and consumptions. Absent of any structural changes in this global economy, its wealth will be drained over time to pay for excessive imports and overconsumptions. Tangible wealth will be transferred gradually from Country C to Countries A and B, producers of raw materials and manufactured goods, respectively.

We will also assume for now that, barring seasonal and anticipated cyclical fluctuations, global production is roughly equal to global consumption. If Country C consistently imports excessively and/or overconsumes, this whole system can be sustained only if the economic values created by Country C (in terms of new equity/debt issuance and/or increase in valuation — this phenomenon will be revisited in Section 3.4) will be sufficient to pay for its imports and continued borrowing. There is nothing inherently wrong with such an approach as long as Country C can demonstrate consistent and exceptional investment skills.

When:

(1) Country C may run up so much debt that the rest of the world loses confidence that it can realistically create sufficient economic values to repay its debts, or
(2) Country C is raising new debt primarily to roll over existing debt and to pay for consumption, or
(3) there is a gradual shifting of high value-added expertise in innovation and investment to Countries A and B,

Country C may have a difficult time issuing equities and debts *ad infinitum*. From that point in time, this global economic structure may become unsustainable.

Alternatively, debt financing can also be seen as a means to create leverage on equity. Debt can be used by Country C to finance its economic value creation process, so it will get to retain a larger share of the total equities that it has issued. Again, this strategy will be sustainable only if the economic value creation process by Country C can outpace the servicing burden on the existing and anticipated (to pay for imports) amounts of debts it raised.

Furthermore, we have assumed that Country A can enjoy more purchasing power initially because of its relative abundance (i.e. it owns the largest share of natural resources available globally), while the model assumes that Countries B and C have equal purchasing power at the outset. (As mentioned earlier, domestic prices of Commodities can be different from country to country even though the same Commodity can be priced in different countries under a single global trade settlement currency.) The model outcome is that Country B will experience asset inflation over time (i.e. cash + investment will outgrow its resource base, given that purchasing power is measured by $PPI(t) = \frac{Cash + Investment}{Commodity}$) while Country C will experience deflationary pressure due to the gradual downsizing of its net assets — *unless* it is able to create sufficient economic values that the increase in the values of its share of equity held can grow faster than the total amount of debts issued. The later scenario is in fact consistent with real-world observations during bull markets in deficit countries.

Another possible unsustainable scenario: What if any potential increase in equity value is not a direct reflection of Country C's ability to innovate, but primarily driven by the demands of SWFs at Countries A and B due to the lack of other sound investment alternatives? At some point, Country C will be unable to justify its equity valuation, and the refusal by the SWFs of Countries A and B to support unreasonable equity valuation may trigger a downward spiral for Country C equities. Since it is *not* in the interest of Countries A and B to force Country C into an abrupt downward spiral, such a mechanism may create a scenario in which Countries A and B are forced to support Country C's continued issuance despite its inability to justify its high equity valuation.

From the perspective of Country C policymakers, they should be concerned if any of the following boundary scenarios (due to unsustainable debts issued by Country C, which will eventually default or be forced into a painful debt restructuring) are reached:

(1) *Scenario 1* — Country C issues more debts/equities (claims by other countries) than it is creating economic values, or the amount of debt becomes so excessive that the market perceives that Country C is raising debts primarily to roll over existing ones and to sustain consumption instead of creating leverage in its capital structure.

(2) *Scenario 2* — SWFs in Countries A and B are investing simply to "buy up" the market, instead of picking sound investments and rewarding companies that create economic values. (This model assumes that only the Investment portion of a country's surplus wealth will be actively managed by a SWF.) In that sense, indexing and indexing *only* by SWFs may create a long-term prob-

lem in that such an investment process typically falls short of incentivizing Country C companies to create economic values by innovation.

Consider the case in which Country C only issues equities, while Countries A and B buy only those equities but no debts. The typical company in Country C will be incentivized to pursue projects that produce stable returns instead of any high-risk, high-return projects (that are more typical among innovation-driven economic value creation). Over time, Country C equities will generate stable but hardly spectacular dividend yields similar to those of preferred stocks or convertible bonds.

There will be minimal practical difference in the outcome of this system as compared to another one supported purely by debt. In the first case, Country C will eventually run out of valuation and revenues to issue new equity (because the valuation/revenue base in any economy that does not emphasize innovation will be relatively low and stable), so Country C will be left with limited means to finance its imports; in the latter case, Country C may be forced into default once it has issued so much debts that servicing the debt load becomes unsustainable, so Countries A and B will simply refuse to buy additional new debts from Country C in the absence of a debt restructuring plan.

(3) *Scenario 3* — Country C issues mostly equity; accordingly, Countries A and B are holding primarily equity. Country C is successful in creating economic values by innovation. However, if the SWFs of Countries A and B only focus on making innovation-driven investments, there is still a significant risk of destabilizing the global economy. The reason is that innovation-driven investments tend to consist of a few "home runs" mixed with plenty of failures.

If Country C goes through a drought period with limited innovations, the SWFs of Countries A and B (as public organizations) may face political pressures to refrain from making additional new investments until some of their existing investments begin to yield credible returns. Their refusal to further invest may cut off the source of funding for Country C to pay for its steady imports/consumptions. That may result in a classic mismatch between income and liability.

Accordingly, it may be unwise for SWFs to hold a high portion of its equity investments in venture capital or private equity to avoid the risk of potentially destabilizing the global financial system, when deficit countries can only rely on the occasional but exceptional yields generated by such investments to pay for its imports. Country C should encourage surplus countries to hold their surpluses in a diversified balance of debt, public equity and private equity/venture capital, in order to better match its refinancing profile, even though SWF investments should aim to incentivize genuine economic value creation processes.

3.3   Potential Outcomes of Policy Interventions

From Section 3.2, our model of the global economy is represented by a system of difference equations (3.7), (3.13) and (3.20):

$$Cash_A (t + 1) + Investment_A (t + 1) = Cash_A (t) + Investment_A (t) + 2.5$$

$$Cash_B (t + 1) + Investment_B (t + 1) = Cash_B (t) + Investment_B (t) + 2.5$$

$$Cash_C (t + 1) + Investment_C (t + 1) - Debt_C (t + 1) - Equity_C (t + 1) =$$
$$Cash_C (t) + Investment_C (t) - Debt_C (t) - Equity_C (t) - 5$$

Bankruptcy of Country C is defined as $Cash_C (t + 1) + Investment_C (t + 1) = 0$, a condition in which Country C runs out of any assets to pay its bills. To avoid reaching bankruptcy, Country C must do one or both of the following:

(1) Issue additional debts so as to increase the amount of cash in hand; or
(2) Make successful investments so that any increase in the valuation and/or dividend yield in its equity holdings will be sufficient to fund its "burn rate".

The first solution (commonly known as "printing money", as well as other clinical descriptions such as quantitative easing) has its limits. Countries A and B are unlikely to buy Country C's bonds indefinitely, when they realize they will only be repaid in a significantly devalued currency (in terms of purchasing power, with an increased monetary base but relative static commodity base), or when Country C's debt load becomes clearly unsustainable, defined as Country C being perceived by the financial markets as having insufficient incoming cashflows to service its existing debts.

The above suggests that the driver to Country C's economic process should be option 2, but option 1 can be used to:

(1) "smooth" potentially volatile valuation and dividend yield payout patterns, or
(2) better match Country C's income-liability profile, or
(3) provide leverage.

It is unrealistic to expect that the financial markets will wait until any country actually reaches bankruptcy. Practically speaking, when $Cash_C (t + 1) + Investment_C (t + 1) < Threshold_C$ (where $Threshold_C$ represents a liquidity level for Country C whereby its debt load can no longer pass sustainability tests commonly accepted by rating and multilateral agencies — for now, we need not be overly concerned about the derivation of $Threshold_C$, except to point out that a liquidity level represented by $Threshold_C$ exists before Country C approaches any *bona fide* solvency difficulties or bankruptcy), the markets will drive up the borrowing cost of Country C by so much to trigger a crisis of market confidence. That will create an adverse impact on Country C's ability to roll over its existing debts.

This section aims to analyze what policy interventions may be carried out to mitigate or even reverse any such crisis of confidence in Country C. Assuming that this model gives a reasonable description of today's global economy, we want to use the model to better understand the potential outcomes of several widely-discussed options in policy intervention.

3.3.1 *Intervention Policy 1 — Restoration of a Gold Standard*

One interpretation of imposing a Gold Standard is to fix Commodity Price Index at a constant K for all countries, i.e. $CPI = \frac{Cash}{Commodity} = K$. Doing so means Country C makes a policy decision one day to fix its currency to K units of commodities. We will assume for simplicity that K will reflect the then prevailing price of Commodity at the point of conversion at time t_1.

At time $t = t_1$, the system of difference equations can be reduced to:

$$K * Commodity_A (t + 1) + Investment_A (t + 1) =$$
$$K * Commodity_A (t) + Investment_A (t) + 2.5 \qquad (3.21)$$

$$K * Commodity_B (t + 1) + Investment_B (t + 1) =$$
$$K * Commodity_B (t) + Investment_B (t) + 2.5 \qquad (3.22)$$

$$K * Commodity_C (t + 1) + Investment_C (t + 1)$$
$$- Debt_C (t + 1) - Equity_C (t + 1) =$$
$$K * Commodity_C (t) + Investment_C (t)$$
$$- Debt_C (t) - Equity_C (t) - 5 \qquad (3.23)$$

From this point on, any new debts issued by Country C will be effectively repaid in Commodity. Assuming fraud risk is negligible (examples of frauds may include: (1) Country C issuing debts with no intention to repay, or (2) Country C makes an accounting misrepresentation that its debt is collateralized by a non-existent/unproven inventory of Commodities) then there is no practical difference between issuing debts and selling Commodities forward.

Now Countries A and B have no reason to buy such debts without Country C pledging its commodity reserves or another form of hard collateral, leaving Country C without any mechanism to borrow simply by "printing money". Under these structural constraints on issuing debts, it will be more logical for Country C to raise funds by issuing as much equity as supported by valuation and revenues linked to any new issuance.

Since equity value will now be measured against a relatively rigid monetary base, any increase in equity value will be tied to actual increase in earnings or productivity (in Commodity terms). Thus, the mandate of the SWFs in Countries A and B become clearer — in any rigidly structured financial markets, there are fewer ways (and therefore opportunities) for SWFs to profit by placing "macro bets" (beta). Their SWFs will need to focus on picking companies that can create values (alpha or stock selection).

If the crisis is created partly by Country C being too aggressive with printing money, such a crisis will deteriorate into a crisis of market confidence that Country C will have difficulties in rolling over the debts that it has already issued. Then, a stable monetary base may restore market confidence or at least do so temporarily, as long as the crisis scenario is a *liquidity* event, defined as one in which Country C will be able to service its debts once market confidence and "normal" level of liquidity return to the market, usually after Country C has shown concrete commitments to pursue the necessary fiscal and budgetary reforms.

However, fixing the size of the monetary base (or making it relatively rigid) will also make it challenging for Country C to raise any additional funds that may be critical to restoring its economic health. If the issue is that this is a *solvency* event (i.e. without new funds, Country C will be driven into bankruptcy), then this is a blunt solution in which one possible undesirable outcome may be the total collapse of Country C's economic activities, since it will have no other way to pay for key imports such as fuel on which the daily functioning of its economy may depend.

Stabilizing the monetary base also makes it unlikely for Countries A and B to accumulate ever-growing public surpluses when Country C simply cannot print IOUs at will. The SWFs of Countries A and B can then focus on managing the legacy of past public surpluses.

3.3.2   *Intervention Policy 2 — "Printing Money"* **Ad Infinitum**

This policy is often given more clinical descriptions such as quantitative easing. The strategy allows the Commodity Price Index to increase in time, so that Commodity Price Index $CPI = \frac{Cash}{Commodity} = K(t) \to \infty$ for large t.

Our global economic system is still consisted of a similar set of equations, except that K is now denoted as a function of time and is generally increasing for $t = t_1$:

$$K(t + 1) * Commodity_A (t + 1) + Investment_A (t + 1) =$$
$$K(t) * Commodity_A (t) + Investment_A (t) + 2.5 \tag{3.24}$$

$$K(t + 1) * Commodity_B (t + 1) + Investment_B (t + 1) =$$
$$K(t) * Commodity_B (t) + Investment_B (t) + 2.5 \tag{3.25}$$

$$K(t + 1) * Commodity_C (t + 1) + Investment_C (t + 1)$$
$$- Debt_C (t + 1) - Equity_C (t + 1) =$$
$$K(t) * Commodity_C (t) + Investment_C (t)$$
$$- Debt_C (t) - Equity_C (t) - 5 \tag{3.26}$$

Country C equity values will drop when dividend discount rates increase (to compensate for the rapid loss of purchasing power by cash). Over time, Commodity will be the one thing that is most likely to hold its value. As in any out-of-control inflationary scenario, the logical response is for Countries A and B to hoard their Commodities and/or delay any exports, so that the goods can fetch as high a price as possible under a rapidly devaluing currency.

The only natural "hedge" available to protect the values of its overall investment holdings is for the SWFs of Countries A and B to allocate to Commodities. (Country A can be less proactive in allocating to commodities since its revenue source is primarily from commodities: the simple alternative is for Country A to export fewer Commodities.) The net effect will be a simultaneous allocation to Commodities by investors, or mass hoarding. Mass hoarding is known to result in distortions in the efficient allocation of economic resources, since Commodity prices will eventually reach a level that hinders productive economic activities. Therefore, it is not obvious how this policy is necessarily helping Country C's economy and the global economy restore their health.

3.3.3 *Intervention Policy 3 — Issuing Alternative Trading Currencies*

Instead of simply letting Country C print money *ad infinitum*, Countries A and B can act to put an end to their monetary union with Country C. At a specific time t_1, Countries A and B may declare that they will create their own common currency to replace Country C's by fixing their common currency to the then prevailing price $K(t_1)$ of commodities, while $K_C(t_1 + \tau)$, $\tau \geq 1$, will continue to fluctuate as a function of time (likely to increase in time), as in:

$$K(t_1) * Commodity_A(t+1) + Investment_A(t+1) =$$
$$K(t_1) * Commodity_A(t) + Investment_A(t) + 2.5 \qquad (3.27)$$

$$K(t_1) * Commodity_B(t+1) + Investment_B(t+1) =$$
$$K(t_1) * Commodity_B(t) + Investment_B(t) + 2.5 \qquad (3.28)$$

$$K_C(t+1) * Commodity_C(t+1) + Investment_C(t+1)$$
$$- Debt_C(t+1) - Equity_C(t+1) =$$
$$K_C(t) * Commodity_C(t) + Investment_C(t)$$
$$- Debt_C(t) - Equity_C(t) - 5 \qquad (3.29)$$

for $t = t_1$. If Country C continues to issue more debts, the new debts will be primarily absorbed by Country C's expanding monetary base, so the net result is for Country C to suffer inflation and rapid devaluation of its domestic currency (relative to the new common currency). Country C will therefore be disincentivized to run up unsustainable levels of debts in such a scenario, although it still has some ability to "print money".

What is not yet modeled in this system is that Country C will eventually lose its ability to import under the pressure of a depreciating currency and its exports are expected to become stronger, thus reducing any imbalance of payments within this global economic system over time. For $t = t_1$, the system can be rewritten as follows:

$$K(t_1) * Commodity_A(t+1) + Investment_A(t+1) =$$
$$K(t_1) * Commodity_A(t) + Investment_A(t) + BalancePayment_A(t) \quad (3.30)$$

$$K(t_1) * Commodity_B(t+1) + Investment_B(t+1) =$$
$$K(t_1) * Commodity_B(t) + Investment_B(t) + BalancePayment_B(t) \quad (3.31)$$

$$K_C(t+1) * Commodity_C(t+1) + Investment_C(t+1)$$
$$- Debt_C(t+1) - Equity_C(t+1) =$$
$$K(t) * Commodity_C(t) + Investment_C(t) - Debt_C(t) - Equity_C(t)$$
$$- BalancePayment_A(t) - BalancePayment_B(t) \qquad (3.32)$$

Barring any extreme scenario in which Country C will reach bankruptcy before the necessary adjustments can be made, it is now feasible for certain structural adjustments to take effects so that the global economy stands a chance to return to some form of equilibrium. This solution is potentially more helpful than simply leaving Country C under the structural constraints of a rigid global Gold Standard, which provides an extremely limited policy toolkit to restore balanced economic growth.

Notice that it is in the interest of Countries A and B to help restore Country C's economy to health; otherwise, their Investments (which are priced in Country C's currency) may rapidly depreciate in value. Moreover, this solution does allow Countries A and B to provide bridge financing for any short-term liquidity scenario. After Countries A and B have exited a monetary union with Country C, the risks for them to purchase any significant amount of Country C debts and equity are: (1) inducing a runaway currency depreciation and domestic asset inflation in Country C without necessarily restoring its economic health; and (2) Countries A and B will be exchanging their new common currency for a potentially depreciating currency, resulting in a form of global economic contagion.

In short, a structural solution by adjusting the relative prices of goods and services appears to be a pre-condition to reversing on-going and persistent imbalances. By comparison, it is unclear how central banks and public surplus managers necessarily have the (effective) monetary and investment tools to solve fiscal and overconsumption challenges. Their intervention is appropriate only when the crisis is clearly a liquidity but not solvency situation; however, it is also notoriously difficult to make any such distinction *ex ante*. Only after Country C finds an effective solution to correct its spending habits, the SWFs of Countries A and B can more effectively deal with the legacy of past imbalances and to invest in Country C's economic recovery.

3.4 Implications to SWF Investing

In this section, we look at how SWFs should operate in real-life asset markets. By now, our audience should understand that the primary mandate of SWFs is to deal with the legacies of past imbalances, instead of using monetary and investment tools to solve fiscal problems. We will explore whether SWFs should stage market rescues to the extent that such rescues may represent healthy long-term investments.

Given various market and global economic realities faced by the investment activities of SWFs, this section aims to answer two specific questions:

(1) SWFs' sheer size can create liquidity shocks to the market if they lead the market to allocate to a certain asset or asset class. When they are ready to sell

such an asset or asset class *en masse*, the likely outcome is that everyone else will follow suit. Thus, their massive size makes any large, directional macro bets at best difficult to execute in practice; in contrast, smaller macro bets may not make much of a difference to the overall profit-and-loss of a SWF, but one wrong macro bet (regardless of size) may result in immediate outcries of misappropriating public funds. Are there rational circumstances for SWFs to consider macro bets?

(2) On one hand, SWF can act as responsible long-term holders to stem temporary runs on specific markets; on the other hand, SWFs do not have infinite resources to respond to *every* liquidity crisis. Can any general principle be identified to guide them so that they are intervening to stem market distortions, instead of providing artificial support to unworthy assets?

3.4.1 *SWF Asset Allocation in Typical Markets*

Accumulating massive reserves in cash or cash equivalent under a rigid currency regime can create potentially destabilizing effects. One possible outcome is to encourage deficit countries to issue bonds until they can no longer afford to roll over their debts. Also, a sustainable deficit country should issue a combination of equities and debts with the goal of creating economic values to pay for its imports and to service its debts. As a result, responsible surplus countries should hold their surpluses in a diversified combination of assets instead of cash and cash equivalent only, a point that has been touched upon by other researchers on SWF investing behavior (see Ang, Goetzmann & Schaefer (2009), Bernstein, Lerner & Schoar (2009), Dyck & Morse (2010), Johan, Knill & Mauck (2011) and Sun & Hesse (2009)). This practical reality gives rise to the need for SWFs to have an appropriate allocation strategy, as well as one that may be different from those suggested by typical asset allocation models due to their size.

We will illustrate our analysis with the net asset representation of Country B.

Net Asset Representation of Country B:

From Equation (3.11) in Section 3.2, we have:

$$NetAsset_B(t) = Cash_B(t) + Commodity_B(t) + Investment_B(t)$$

Similarly,

$$NetAsset_B(t+1) = Cash_B(t+1) + Commodity_B(t+1) + Investment_B(t+1)$$
$$(3.33)$$

As an enhancement to Equation (3.11) now that both the valuations and the allocations of Country B's assets may be changed, we have:

$$NetAsset_B (t + 1) - NetAsset_B (t) =$$
$$NetExport_B (t) + \Delta Cash_B (t, t + 1)$$
$$+ \Delta Commodity_B (t, t + 1) + \Delta Investment_B (t, t + 1) \quad (3.34)$$

where

$$\Delta Commodity_B (t, t + 1)$$
$$= Price_{Commodity} (t + 1) * Wt_{Commodity} (t + 1)$$
$$- Price_{Commodity} (t) * Wt_{Commodity} (t)$$
$$= Price_{Commodity} (t + 1) * Wt_{Commodity} (t + 1)$$
$$- Price_{Commodity} (t + 1) * Wt_{Commodity} (t)$$
$$+ Price_{Commodity} (t + 1) * Wt_{Commodity} (t)$$
$$- Price_{Commodity} (t) * Wt_{Commodity} (t)$$
$$= Price_{Commodity} (t + 1) * \Delta Wt_{Commodity} (t, t + 1)$$
$$+ Return_{Commodity} (t + 1, t) * Wt_{Commodity} (t) \quad (3.35)$$

Analogous equations similar to Equation (3.35) can be derived for Cash and Investment, respectively. Notice that these portfolio weights can be thought of as unit holdings normalized to a specific point in time, which is a standard notation used in asset management. In other words, Equation (3.34) can be rewritten as:

$$NetAsset_B (t + 1) - NetAsset_B (t)$$
$$= NetExport_B (t) + \Delta Allocation_B(t, t + 1) + \Delta Valuation_B (t, t + 1)$$
$$(3.36)$$

where

$$\Delta Allocation_B (t, t + 1) = Price_{Cash} (t + 1) * \Delta Wt_{Cash} (t, t + 1)$$
$$+ Price_{Commodity} (t + 1) * \Delta Wt_{Commodity} (t, t + 1)$$
$$+ Price_{Investment} (t + 1) * \Delta Wt_{Investment} (t, t + 1)$$
$$(3.37)$$

and

$$\Delta Valuation_B (t, t + 1) = Return_{Cash} (t, t + 1) * Wt_{Cash} (t)$$
$$+ Return_{Commodity} (t, t + 1) * Wt_{Commodity} (t)$$
$$+ Return_{Investment} (t, t + 1) * Wt_{Investment} (t)$$
$$(3.38)$$

Moreover, since the net sum of any *changes* in weights due to a specific allocation decision at a specific point in time must sum to zero, i.e:

$$\Delta Wt_{Cash}(t, t+1) + \Delta Wt_{Commodity}(t, t+1) + \Delta Wt_{Investment}(t, t+1) = 0 \quad (3.39)$$

Accordingly, Equation (3.37) can be rewritten as:

$$\begin{aligned}
&\Delta Allocation_B(t, t+1) \\
&= Price_{Cash}(t+1) * \left(-\Delta Wt_{Commodity}(t, t+1) - \Delta Wt_{Investment}(t, t+1)\right) \\
&\quad + Price_{Commodity}(t+1) * \Delta Wt_{Commodity}(t, t+1) \\
&\quad + Price_{Investment}(t+1) * \Delta Wt_{Investment}(t, t+1) \\
&= \left(Price_{Commodity}(t+1) - Price_{Cash}(t+1)\right) * \Delta Wt_{Commodity}(t, t+1) \\
&\quad + (Price_{Investment}(t+1) - Price_{Cash}(t+1)) * \Delta Wt_{Investment}(t, t+1)
\end{aligned}$$

$$(3.40)$$

Based on the relationships derived above, investment performance is determined by two terms: the change in allocation ($\Delta Allocation_B$) as well as the change in valuation ($\Delta Valuation_B$) of each asset.

Allocating to an appreciating asset (relative to cash) is almost always positive. However, because of their size, SWFs can "buy up" specific market segments, which may be accompanied by a move in the opposite direction when they must eventually "cash out". That means that it is only effective for SWFs to make long-term macro bets based on price changes that reflect fundamental changes in relative market values as a result of economic value creation.

Nothing in the $\Delta Valuation_B$ and $\Delta Allocation_B$ terms penalizes a SWF for making a long-term investment as long as such an investment can beat cash returns at the time of exit. As a result, SWFs are in positions to pick companies, industry sectors or market segments that create long-term values or reflect fundamental changes in market values (commonly known as "alpha investing"). Their ability to hold onto their investments for much longer horizons than typical pensions and endowments (given the lack of any explicit liability terms) can provide them with significant advantages in the competition for capital. In contrast, passive indexing (commonly known as "beta investing") does not necessarily incentivize economic value creation, and does not automatically help SWFs realize their investment goals over the long-term horizon.

Specifically, because there are other terms such as $NetExport_B$ in the national balance sheet (as well as other yet-to-be-specified terms such as *Government Surplus*), professional managers in SWFs should be incentivized to pick not just valued-added investments, but also companies and sectors that complement existing profiles of national outputs.

In view of the above, we can name one real-life example of an ineffective SWF investment: SWFs of oil exporters investing in companies active in oil services, which is a surprisingly common practice among oil-exporting surplus countries. We can also name a real-life example of an effective SWF investment: SWF investing in rare-earth metals by analyzing fundamental supply and demand and technology trends.

3.4.2 SWF Allocation under Market in Distress

As mentioned, the financial markets may go into distress when

$$Cash_C(t) + Investment_C(t) < Threshold_C$$

Specifically, when the total returns (both yield and valuation) on cash and investments earned by Country C are smaller than its net outflows, investors are likely to respond by demanding punitive yields on Country C's new debts issued.

In that case, when will it be appropriate for SWFs to step in?

Case 1:

The investments held by Country C have sound fundamentals, but they are yielding below average returns because of prevailing economic headwinds. Long-term returns are expected to be able to fund Country C's outflows, so this is primarily a liquidity situation.

In most economic downturns, the second and the third terms in $\Delta Valuation_B$ are expected to be negative:

$$\Delta Valuation_B(t, t+1)$$
$$= Return_{Cash}(t, t+1) * Wt_{Cash}(t)$$
$$+ Return_{Commodity}(t, t+1) * Wt_{Commodity}(t)$$
$$+ Return_{Investment}(t, t+1) * Wt_{Investment}(t)$$

$$(3.41)$$

In order to intervene, SWFs need to lock in losses in Commodity and Investment and reallocate those assets to Cash in order to fund a rescue attempt. Since $\Delta Allocation_B$ is given by:

$$\Delta Allocation_B(t, t+1)$$
$$= \left(Price_{Commodity}(t+1) - Price_{Cash}(t+1)\right) * \Delta Wt_{Commodity}(t, t+1)$$
$$+ (Price_{Investment}(t+1) - Price_{Cash}(t+1)) * \Delta Wt_{Investment}(t, t+1)$$

$$(3.42)$$

Both $\Delta Wt\,(t, t+1)$ terms can be negative in order to raise cash to fund a rescue. Intervention will be appropriate when the SWF portfolio manager expects that $Price_{Cash}\,(t+1) \gg Price_{Commodity}\,(t+1)$ and/or $Price_{Cash}\,(t+1) \gg Price_{Investment}\,(t+1)$, and do so by a significant amount. The decision to raise cash under the circumstances suggests that:

(1) it is better to "unload" risky assets and invest in cash instruments if the expectation is that market will further collapse; and
(2) *without* a rescue, both $Return_{Commodity}\,(t, t+1)$ and $Return_{Investment}\,(t, t+1)$ may suffer so badly that on balance it is still in the interest of a SWF to participate in a rescue effort in order to support valuations in the rest of its portfolio.

Similar arguments were used to launch the rescues of certain global banks by syndicates of SWFs in 2008.

Case 2:

If Country C's ability to generate cash is still a long way from meeting outflows purely from debt servicing cost, then the situation should be interpreted as a solvency situation. SWFs should demand debt restructuring as discussed in Section 3.3 before making further investments in Country C's debts.

This is similar to arguments used by some SWFs for their reluctance to participate in the capital infusion of the European Financial Stability Fund in 2010.

3.4.3   *SWF Participation in Rescue Efforts*

The reality is that there is no hard and fast rule for any SWF to separate Case 1 from Case 2, just like no central bank has identified a clear signal to distinguish a liquidity situation from a solvency crisis. More often than not, a liquidity crisis may simply deteriorate into a solvency crisis, similar to how any self-fulfilling prophecy unfolds, when countries in distress face further attacks from speculators. Once borrowing costs rise dramatically, Country C will no longer be able to roll over its existing debts and pay its bills. At the same time, the economic collapse of Country C may eventually hurt Countries A and B. So, when should a SWF step in and participate in a rescue effort?

Multi-period analysis from time t to $t + \tau$ gives rise to an inequality condition that appears similar to those found in stochastic control problems. Please note that

Price (t) of different assets are stochastic variables in the relationships below:

$$NetAsset_B(t + \tau) - NetAsset_B(t)$$

$$= \sum_{i=0}^{\tau-1} \left\{ \begin{array}{l} NetExport_B(t + i) \\ + \Delta Allocation_B(t + i, t + i + 1) \\ + \Delta Valuation_B(t + i, t + i + 1) \end{array} \right\}$$

$$> 0$$

$$(3.43)$$

Expanding on the $\Delta Allocation_B$ and $\Delta Valuation_B$ terms give rise to the following inequality:

$$NetAsset_B(t + \tau) - NetAsset_B(t)$$

$$= \sum_{i=0}^{\tau-1} \left\{ \begin{array}{l} NetExport_B(t) \\ + \left[Price_{Commodity}(t + i + 1) - Price_{Cash}(t + i + 1) \right] \\ \quad * \Delta Wt_{Commodity}(t + i, t + i + 1) \\ + [Price_{Investment}(t + i + 1) - Price_{Cash}(t + i + 1)] \\ \quad * \Delta Wt_{Investment}(t + i, t + i + 1) \\ + Return_{Cash}(t + i, t + i + 1) * Wt_{Cash}(t + i) \\ + Return_{Commodity}(t + i, t + i + 1) * Wt_{Commodity}(t + i) \\ + Return_{Investment}(t + i, t + i + 1) * Wt_{Investment}(t + i) \end{array} \right\}$$

$$> 0 \qquad\qquad (3.44)$$

Intervention may be desirable when this inequality is satisfied.

Analysis:

SWFs are likely to suffer *initially* as a result of participating in a rescue: they can only sell Commodities and Investments in a rapid declining market in order to fund any rescue attempt.

If there is a successful rescue in a market crisis, SWFs have the ability to benefit from "sell high, buy low" in the $\Delta Allocation_B$ summation term. Once the rescue effort has turned the situation around, SWFs can liquidate its cash and reallocate to Commodities and Investments at market lows. In integral form, $\Delta Wt_{Commodity}(t + i, t + i + 1)$ and $\Delta Wt_{Investment}(t + i, t + i + 1)$ are negative when $Price_{Commodity}(t + i + 1)$ and $Price_{Investment}(t + i + 1)$ collapse, but (depending on the specific timing of sound investment decisions) both terms can be positive when prices recover.

Realistically, one should expect that the $\Delta Valuation_B$ term may suffer because not all investments will come out intact in most financial crises, so failed investments will still impact the balance sheets of SWFs. When converted from discrete time to integral form, the terms

$$Return_{Cash}(t+i, t+i+1) * Wt_{Cash}(t+i)$$

$$+ Return_{Commodity}(t+i, t+i+1) * Wt_{Commodity}(t+i)$$

$$+ Return_{Investment}(t+i, t+i+1) * Wt_{Investment}(t+i)$$

may not show strong directions either way — most investments will recover, but some may simply experience total or significant losses.

As long as $NetExport_B(t)$ can still break even or even become slightly positive after all is said and done, a SWF has done its job in stabilizing the markets. From a self-interest viewpoint, Country B may not want to force Country C into any disorderly defaults because the $NetExport_B(t)$ term may not recover after a disorderly default, and there is no guarantee that the values of its Investments will hold up after Country C goes into default. In contrast, Country A may be less concerned because it is endowed with Commodities, as long as Commodity exports are sufficiently inelastic.

Several practical implementation issues will include the following:

(1) In practice, it is not realistic to expect any portfolio manager to be able to pick any market "highs" and "lows" in order to maximize the $\Delta Allocation_B$ term. There can also be a significant loss in $\Delta Valuation_B$ during the initial phase of any rescue effort. Naturally, it does not help if the initial losses taken by a SWF to participate in a rescue attempt are so huge that it may destabilize or even topple a government in power. SWFs must be realistic about the size of the losses that they are prepared to absorb. This is consistent with the steep losses and subsequent rebound experienced by some SWFs after 2008, which is a natural result of SWFs' stabilization role, but nonetheless creates significant political difficulties for the governments concerned.

(2) Unlike in classical mechanics, markets do not obey any fixed laws of nature. In theory, given the inequality condition in Equation (3.44), one can model a potential rescue effort by using Bellman's method or other stochastic control solver to obtain a stochastically optimal solution as markets evolve in real time (e.g. similar techniques are commonly used in flight guidance systems), but, unlike in aerodynamics, market shocks are at best difficult to predict and calibrate. In engineering terms, stochastic control methods are not necessarily reliable when solving stochastic control problems with large, "uncontrolled" jumps such as those observed in real-life markets. Therefore, it may be unwise for SWFs to overly rely on complex and opaque mathematical models, instead of using a parsimonious model constructed with straightforward mathematics to guide sound investment judgment.

(3) For SWFs to step in, the general pre-condition should be that the situation is a liquidity not solvency crisis. Since the situation is driven by liquidity (and therefore confidence), markets do need to be convinced that any rescue attempt will be of a sufficient size that it can mitigate or even reverse any such crisis of market confidence. Feeble attempts to intervene (however sound the mathematical derivations) can only make the perception of a bad situation worse: if the SWFs cannot reverse the crisis, the net effect is for these SWFs to lock in more losses by raising cash in a collapsing market, thereby using up "dry powders" to launch credible rescue attempts in the future and shaking up market confidence further.

3.5 Summary

The proposed approach of this chapter emphasizes on:

(1) parsimonious modeling, by focusing on modeling the flows and constraints in the global economy instead of overlaying complex constraints and/or impact models on top of a sophisticated asset allocation model;
(2) providing a reasonable description that is roughly consistent with the current state of the global economy and a plausible explanation of known investment behavior among SWFs in the recent past; and
(3) laying the foundation for a continuous-time framework for future research.

This chapter aims to illustrate only the general framework used by the proposed approach. Any real-world implementation is expected to go beyond SWF investing to incorporate other macro drivers in the global economy, such as open market operations by central banks and government fiscal policies, with the model calibrated based on macroeconomic statistics. The practical issue is how to do so without introducing excessive degrees of freedom. It may be impractical to address that level of details in any single model.

Policy insights (see related discussions in Lee (2011a), Lee (2011b) and Lee (2011c)) related to SWF investing gained from this chapter include:

(1) SWFs are artifacts of global imbalances. Neither returning to a rigid Gold Standard nor allowing deficit economies to issue debts or print money *ad infinitum* is a constructive solution. Another "shock therapy" is for resource-rich and exporting countries to create their own common currency to force deficit economies to instill fiscal disciplines. These solutions can cause unintended

adverse consequences in theory, and they may come with potentially unmanageable execution risk in practice.

(2) It is not obvious how SWFs, as major concentrations of public wealth, are better equipped than central banks and multilateral monetary agencies to deal with solvency situations. However, they can step in to help resolve liquidity crises, before any such situation deteriorates irreparably as in a self-fulfilling prophecy. SWFs also need to be realistic about the amount of losses that they can absorb, at least during the initial stages of any rescue attempts, before destabilizing even toppling governments.

(3) SWFs can play a role in stabilizing the markets. From a self-interest point of view, export-driven surplus economies may be ill-advised to force deficit economies into any disorderly defaults, because the net exports terms on their national balance sheets may not recover after any such disorderly defaults, while there is no reason to believe that the values of their investments will necessarily hold up after disorderly defaults. In contrast, resource-rich countries can afford to be less concerned because they are endowed with commodities, as long as those exports are sufficiently inelastic.

Chapter 4

Future Directions

4.1 Evolving Global Financial Landscape

4.1.1 *Euro Crisis in Slow Motion*

One only needs to put the size of the distressed European economies in context in order to appreciate the scale of the Euro debt crisis and why it is perhaps the single largest threat to today's global economy.

According to the International Monetary Fund (IMF), the 2011 nominal GDP of the European Union (EU) is about US$17.6 trillion versus US$15.1 trillion for the United States (US). Ireland has a GDP of about US$218 billion, or about the size of US state Louisiana; Portugal about US$239 billion, or about that of Connecticut; Greece and Cyprus about US$328 billion, putting them somewhere between Maryland and Michigan; finally, Spain about US$1.49 trillion, or roughly a combination of Texas, Mississippi and Oklahoma. These numbers fluctuate according to foreign exchange rates.

Roughly speaking, the "distressed" European economies represent 15% of the EU economy. If one includes Italy given the size of its public debts relative to GDP, then "troubled" economies represent about 27% of the EU economy. The obvious concern is not just about Spain or Greece, but potential snowball effects.

Germany represents 20% of EU GDP, which is similar to the rough percentage represented by the New York and Californian economies out of the US total. Like in the case of New York and California, there is a natural limit to what Germany can achieve with its 20% share, if a significant portion of the EU economy goes into serious distress.

Europe's temporary bailout mechanism, the European Financial Stability Facility (EFSF), has an authorized borrowing capacity of 440 billion euros. Based on rough headline estimates, 78 billion euros has been committed to Portugal, 85 billion euros to Ireland, two packages of 240 billion euros to Greece, and another estimated 100 billion euros to Spain. Cyprus may eventually require as much as 20 billion euros, which is roughly its banking system's exposures to Greece.

Although not all European financial rescue attempts will be funded by the EFSF, the existing rescue packages sum to 523 billion euros, which already exceeds the authorized borrowing capacity of EFSF at 440 billion euros. That is one likely explanation why EFSF faced multiple rating agency downgrades in the summer of 2013[1].

Clearly, EFSF does not have much surplus capacity left for another EU country in crisis, or to boost an existing rescue package. Its permanent successor program the European Stability Mechanism (ESM) began operations on 8 October 2012 as a replacement of EFSF, which was set to expire as a rescue facility as of 1 July 2013[2].

"Sound economies" in the EU simply don't have infinite resources. In the absence of other effective policy tools, one way out is for the European Central Bank (ECB) to "print" more euros to fund rescue attempts.

Voters in typical political processes respond in months, but markets can "vote with their feet" within hours if the ECB puts its credibility on the line. Policy makers need to face down the fear of creating self-fulfilling prophecies by "gaming out" key scenarios, in order to identify actionable solutions.

Last-minute Greek and Cypriot votes might have averted immediate disasters. However, if the electorates of the PIIGS countries (acronym used to describe Portugal, Italy, Ireland, Greece and Spain) continue to "fester", eventually residents of these countries may rush to transfer euros out of their domestic banking systems, artificially inducing bank runs. The ECB will then be forced to step up replacing the deposits of failing domestic banks.

There may be a point at which the ECB may refuse to inject further liquidity in order to "firewall" the rest of the Euro zone, one possible unpleasant scenario described by Gavyn Davies, former chief economist at Goldman Sachs and former economic policy adviser to the British Government.

Any messy exit may require the overnight freezing of deposits at domestic banks and subsequently forced conversions to new local currencies. Domestic central banks may be asked to take over the liquidity injection operations from the ECB.

---

[1]See http://www.reuters.com/article/2012/01/16/us-eurozone-efsf-sp-idUSTRE80F10V20120116 and http://www.reuters.com/article/2013/07/15/fitch-downgrades-european-financial-stab-idUSFit66360220130715.

[2]See http://www.efsf.europa.eu/about/index.htm.

To avoid systemic failures, new currencies will need to stay within narrow trading bands against the Euro under some form of capital control, such as a currency board mechanism.

Since the administrative process of printing any new currencies will be non-trivial, the domestic economies will barely function with "underground" euros. Affected economies will shrink significantly because of capital control as well as disappearing investors, and perhaps even tourists concerned about public unrest.

A currency board mechanism can survive only if it is backed by the ECB, at least so temporarily, costing billions more with little hope of recovering from earlier bailout packages.

Fearing catastrophic outcomes from exiting the euro, PIIGS voters support their countries' austerity drives to stay in the Euro zone. However, it is expected to take years for some Governments to emerge from effective bankruptcies. In the meantime, PIIGS electorates will continue to fester over growth solutions every now and then, adding to potentially unproductive public sector spending and the weight of public debts.

As economic fundamentals continue to diverge between the Euro-zone core and its periphery, there will be angry finger-pointing among Euro-zone core voters who had disagreed with the fiscal pact. It will be at best arduous to come to any near-term solutions on potential ways to finance further fiscal expansions.

In the meantime, wages and prices in PIIGS countries continue to be uncompetitive. Without any flexible exchange rate mechanism for making necessary adjustments, investors stay away from economies running on an "overvalued" currency.

The only good news? Bankrupted economies are now less likely to infect banks in the Euro-zone core. However, with some of their key customers in economic distress, Euro-zone core economies also have a difficult time recovering. Only when Euro-zone core countries begin to recover, PIIGS countries can begin to work their way out of the economic mess.

The likely economic outcome is not a pleasant scenario. In fact, investor George Soros made the following blunt assessments at the Festival of Economics held at Trento, Italy, on 2 June 2012[3]:

> By the end of March this year the Bundesbank had claims of some 660 billion euros against the central banks of the periphery countries... The Bundesbank has become aware of the potential danger. It is now engaged in a campaign against the indefinite expansion of the money supply and it has started taking measures to limit the losses it would sustain in case of a breakup. This is creating a

---

[3] See http://www.georgesoros.com/interviews-speeches/entry/remarks_at_the_festival_of_economics_trento_italy/.

self-fulfilling prophecy. Once the Bundesbank starts guarding against a breakup everybody will have to do the same.

Here are some additional cold facts. The growing silence among German policymakers and influential economists on the euro breakup issue suggests that German policymakers may have transitioned from a "search and rescue" mission into a recovery operation. Furthermore, German news magazine *Der Spiegel* reported that the EU has begun planning for an "economic government and a true fiscal union"[4], but it seems rather unlikely that all Euro-zone countries can meet the economic conditions to stay in such a fiscal union.

Eventually, the ECB may turn to drastic measures in order to "manage" the inevitable exits by certain peripheral EU countries. Taxpayers somewhere within the Euro-zone will have to pay, or external entities with trillion-dollar balance sheets will need to inject funds into the Euro-zone.

Observers argue that the Germans and northern Europeans should pay their way out of the mess. The ugly alternative is that they may be left with unenforceable claims (a legacy of the ECB Payment Mechanism) against the Euro-zone periphery estimated at a trillion euros.

4.1.2   *Impacts on Third-Party Bystanders*

Given the macroeconomic analysis in the last subsection, this subsection wants to better understand the potential impacts on "third-party bystanders" — the surplus economies around the world, particularly those in East Asia and the Middle East, as well as their SWFs that are holding the euro as one of their main reserve currencies.

One probable consequence is that they may suffer significant losses from a dramatic devaluation. Instead of leaving their euro reserves at the mercy of the ECB, surplus economies can consider the alternative of active participation in a rescue effort. As an example, Singapore has first-hand experience in facing the political fallout from bailing out international banks in troubles.

The Reality? Financial theories are much cleaner than executing real-life transactions in distressed markets. Essentially, the rescuer will be buying in a collapsing market, without knowing when they can recover their funds. Local voters are unlikely to appreciate the bigger global picture, resulting in public outcries over the "waste" of public funds.

---

[4]See   http://www.spiegel.de/international/europe/why-germany-must-give-up-power-to-save-the-euro-a-837063.html.

There are benefits for surplus countries like Singapore to participate in future EU rescue efforts. First, the rescue can steer countries in distress away from economic collapse, which may lead to a global economic depression. Second, the rescuer may avoid a rapid devaluation of its reserves. Finally, under an effective deal structure, the rescuer may get something in return for its "investment".

One possible rescue scenario can be the following:

(1) The ESM can create a mechanism by which SWFs in surplus countries can invest in the recovery of economies in distress, allowing the ESM to recycle its capital;
(2) Such a mechanism can work closely with the IMF, but politically this is likely to require a separate mechanism independent of the IMF, as long as Europeans continue to be in charge of the IMF; and
(3) Otherwise, there will be a commercially unacceptable situation in which the debtors will be placed in charge of their own creditor's committee, making it infeasible to encourage serious participation by Asian and Middle Eastern SWFs.

The general idea is to create a special purpose vehicle by "repackaging" ESM loans into collateralized papers to be sold to SWFs in surplus economies, so as to free up the ESM balance sheet for future rescues. Only then, the European rescue mechanisms will have sufficient funds (and therefore the necessary credit rating) to restore credibility in the market.

Rescue loans should continue to be made to countries and countries only, and they will rank among their most senior debts. When a country disperses emergency funds to its banks, the banks should issue preferred shares as collateral. Such collaterals are in turn placed within the special purpose vehicle to sweeten the yields for "distressed bond" investors. As a precondition for participation, the ECB may need to agree upfront on the explicit condition for not funding future rescues by "printing" euros or other forms of indefinite monetary expansion.

The Euro-zone will also need to keep its house in order by planning for the orderly departure of certain Euro-zone countries in unsustainable fiscal situations. As long as the ECB is willing to announce the explicit conditions triggering an orderly exit, peripheral Euro-zone voters will get to choose whether they want to stay or go. As a hypothetical example, an orderly exit of Greece can be managed in the following way:

(1) The ECB and the Bank of Greece can jointly manage the exchange rate of the new drachma against the euro for say one year. A narrow trading band

is allowed under a currency board mechanism. Doing so gives the market a chance to find a suitable level for trading the new drachma, before allowing free trading and lifting capital control.

(2) Greek-based euro savings will be allowed to stay in euros to pre-empt an artificial bank run, but with the appropriate incentives to encourage their eventual conversion into the new drachma. Euro debts in Greece will be converted into the new drachma at its future exchange rate one-year ahead.

(3) The Greek Government will mandate all domestic payments to be made in the new drachma, but with an initial grace period for allowing certain settlements in euros, due to the expected administrative delays in any physical currency conversion scheme.

Unlike the credit crunch in 2008, Asian policymakers have learned to minimize the potential impact from any "freezing up" in trading and financing relationships. Central banks around the world now have gained access to contingency policy tools if they must respond.

The US dollar is also far more important as a funding currency than the euro. Overall, the Euro crisis has a lesser risk of causing immediate damages to the real economies in surplus countries.

However, the longer-term ramifications can be much deeper, since the numbers involved are significantly bigger. This crisis is about country or even countries, not just one or two investment banks. The uncertainty will be much larger with the potential for creating long-term global economic malaise. Therefore, there are still credible risks to relatively open Asian economies such as Singapore. US growth is likely to continue its "stop and go" pattern except in its key innovation areas such as information technology and bio-technology. Europe may take years to work out its problems. Asia must do more to help than simply avoiding past mistakes.

According to a research report published by DBS Group Research, by 2016 Asia-10 GDP will equal to that of the US, and by 2020 Asia will be putting 2.5 times more new demand on the global table than the US, becoming twice the economic driver the US is[5].

Asia needs to realize that it is playing an increasingly important role in balancing the global economy. Asian SWFs ought to be prepared to preempt another potential global financial meltdown and ultimately an economic collapse.

---

[5]See http://www.dbs.com/TreasuresPrivateClient/Documents/PDF/DBS_IMAGING_ ASIA_2020.pdf.

4.2 Thinking Ahead

Which economic scenarios may matter the most to a typical SWF over its medium-term planning horizon? What may happen if any such extreme scenario becomes a reality? Is there any mitigation technique that can be deployed, or any asset allocation that can help buffer the potential shock?

In this section, we will attempt to answer these questions with asset-level econometric analyses. It is important to note that, like all econometric models, industrial-strength models are constantly being updated. Our goal in this section is to illustrate the methodologies proposed. Please note that these analyses are provided as numerical examples, but that they should not be relied on for making any investment decisions.

We will avoid excessive mathematical details in this section. Its goal is to illustrate the proposed methodology and provide helpful examples on interpreting its outputs. Although any market, model and portfolio data used in this illustration are collected from real market sources, the author has deliberately avoided naming any specific dates and estimation intervals used, so that it is absolutely clear that the focus of this section is about methodology instead of specific numerical results.

4.2.1 *Scenario 1 — Default of Major Debt Issuer*

When a major debtor country fails to honor its debts, resulting in chaos in the global currency and interest rate markets, will such an event trigger a global economic meltdown among even the surplus countries, now that their foreign currency reserves and sovereign wealth funds may be worth significantly less than before?

Despite the ongoing political brinkmanship over the US Federal Government budget, repercussions from the much talked about US dollar default scenario and any reduced financing flexibility may still be overly politicized. After all, the US Government issues its debts in US dollars, and the US Treasury still has a long list of "extraordinary measures" at its disposal[6]. A potentially more problematic scenario is a default by a country such as Italy, which US\$2.9 trillion in debts is the world's third largest after the US and Japan[7], with both of them enjoying the luxury of issuing debts in their own domestic currencies that they fully control. Global markets will gyrate amid fears of an Italian default.

---

[6]The full list of "extraordinary measures" can be found at http://gao.gov/products/GAO-12-701.

[7]See http://www.telegraph.co.uk/finance/economics/10139939/Italy-could-need-EU-rescue-within-six-months-warns-Mediobanca.html.

Table 4.1   Factor Shocks in Scenario 1 — Default of Major Debt Issuer

Factor	Shock	Before	After
Euro STOXX 50	-15%	2816.88	2394.35
CAC	-11%	4064.32	3617.08
DAX	-4%	8318.32	7985.59
Euro Govn't 2-Year Yield	+155%	0.169%	0.431%
EURUSD	-18%	1.3310	1.0914
Gold	+20%	1312.65	1575.57

Please refer to Table 4.1 for such a scenario. The idea is that a significant meltdown in southern Europe will drive down their stock markets as well as the Euro STOXX. Euro government bond yields will jump. Euro will reach close to parity against the US Dollar, while Gold will revert to levels seen during the worst days of the Euro-zone crisis. Based on this scenario, a mock Temasek portfolio (constructed by using public holdings information) would incur a loss of just over -20%. While a SWF may be able to hedge out any immediate market impact, the more relevant issue is that the portfolio is likely to suffer from longer-term economic malaise that may result from a potential disintegration of the Euro-zone.

4.2.2   Scenario 2 — Mass Hoarding of Commodities

If the sovereign wealth funds of every surplus country rush into taking long positions in commodities, the net result will be a form of mass hoarding, which will drive up prices of commodities and leave impoverished millions without ready access to food and fuel. The most likely commodity factor to be driven up will be crude oil given its liquidity. Such a scenario can be induced by a geological "surprise", i.e. a market rumor that known oil reserves that were once thought to be accessible turns out to be significantly more costly to extract than estimated.

Our specific goal is to model a market event and one that is probably linked to geopolitical shocks, instead of any production-driven long-term economic event. In order to fully understand the longer-term economic impact of a sharp reduction in oil production, it will be necessary to model out the entire supply and demand chain of petrochemicals to study the full impact on production and consumption patterns. What we are interested in is a plausible "mark to market" event. We find it helpful to use the shocks from the OPEC oil embargo as guidance (see Table 4.2).

Table 4.2   Factor Shocks in Scenario 2 — Mass Hoarding of Commodities

Factor	Shock	Before	After
Brent Crude	+132.50%	109.36	254.26

Under such a scenario, our mock Temasek portfolio will incur a loss of about -27%. We have found that the Temasek portfolio has a 6-month beta of about 0.37 to the Rogers International Commodity Index (RICI). In other words, just to break even, Temasek will need a long RICI exposure of about US$64 billion, while the assets under management of the entire RICI ETF is only about US$630 million (or less than 1% of the total required). This provides one plausible explanation why non-mineral SWFs have not piled into commodities, despite the fact that a significant commodity exposure appears to be a good complement to some of the relevant national balance sheets.

4.2.3 Scenario 3 — Conflicts in East Asia

Although the Japanese markets have seen a recent period of strength on the back of "Abenomics", its economic future remains cloudy with unresolved geopolitical tensions with Japan's immediate neighbors and key economic partners.

On the Korean peninsula, North Korea has reportedly warned that Tokyo will be its first target if Japan maintains its "hostile posture" to intercept North Korean test missiles. Given the unproven targeting capabilities of North Korean nuclear missiles, North Korea could decide to launch a high-altitude electromagnetic pulse (EMP) attack on Japan, which would cause economic damage so extensive that it could cripple the nation's tightly-knitted supply chain even with limited civilian casualties.

In another potential geopolitical flash point in the same region, continued escalation of the Diaoyu/Senkaku Islands dispute between China and Japan drew heightened tension in 2012. China and Japan are the world's second and third largest economies respectively and top bilateral trading partners, with China as the biggest destination for Japanese exports. Starting in 2013, hardline rhetoric escalated into regular scrambling of fighter jets and massive naval maneuvering by both sides. Japanese firms would struggle to find alternatives that offer similar competitive labor and production costs while losing their largest export market. Consequently, any military incidents (whether intentional or accidental) could negatively impact Japan's economy and investment environment.

We have constructed in Table 4.3 a market scenario that reflects the possibility of restrained skirmishes.

Under such a scenario, our mock Temasek portfolio will incur a loss of about -11%. This is a scenario in which there is one simple and effective mitigation technique available by allocating away from Japan as well as any companies with significant exposures to Japan (e.g. banks, transportation, real estate developers with significant exposures to the Japanese economy).

Table 4.3   Factor Shocks in Scenario 3 — Conflicts in East Asia

Factor	Shock	Before	After
TOPIX	-11.00%	1139.59	1014.24
JGB 10-Year Yield	-23.00%	0.760%	0.585%
USDJPY	+14.00%	97.03	110.61
Gold	+4.50%	1312.65	1371.72

4.3   Investment Policy Implications

4.3.1   *Surplus Countries*

The investment policy implications to surplus countries are as follows:

(1) *Combining passive and active management* — If sovereign wealth managers of all surplus countries simply aim to achieve market returns instead of firm-specific returns, a standard investment thesis given the combined size of their holdings, doing so will steer the world's surplus capital toward established firms, in effect driving capital away from innovative and potentially higher productivity ventures. If all SWFs decide to go passive, that will be bad news for the global economy, since innovation requires venture-style entrepreneurship typically not achievable by R&D spending made by bureaucratic large-capitalization companies alone.

(2) *A consistent risk and return attribution framework that can be explained to the public* — Like large commercial asset management operations, SWFs can benefit from having a consistent investment framework to demystify the asset allocation process for their governmental clients and the people whom they are investing on behalf of. Investment professionals at each level should be incentivized to maximize active returns for their governmental clients. Likewise, more senior professionals should be asked to "own" the allocation of capital among asset classes and sub-asset classes.

(3) *Encourage focus on at least medium-term results* — It is often impossible to make drastic changes to SWF portfolios over the short-term. Economic views, estimates on factor shocks, risk and performance attributions as well as employee incentives should be based on a pragmatic medium-term estimation horizon of say 5 years. Otherwise, one possible outcome is that investment professionals will be incentivized to take short-term risks by using the typical size of a SWF to "buy up" the market in order to receive handsome year-end bonuses, only to crash the markets of those specific assets when the SWF must eventually cash out.

(4) *Don't be bashful about scenario and contingency planning* — Typical hedge fund managers tend to think of themselves as being able to hedge out exposures that may have gone wrong "on the spot" with sheer bravado. Given the size of most SWFs, the ability to do so will be at best wishful thinking. Of course, putting together the analytical infrastructure to support portfolios of such a size will be painstaking. Suffice it to say that there is no harm in conducting "planning drills" for all plausible scenarios and contingencies, since SWF portfolios cannot be turned "on a dime".

(5) *SWFs can no longer afford to say that the global economy is someone else's problem* — First, most SWFs are required to invest outside their domestic economies. If the global economy crashes, their portfolios are likely to suffer along with everyone else's portfolio. Second, our analysis above shows that the most difficult risk for any SWF to hedge against is the risk of a potential global financial meltdown. Since SWFs are in the position to take preemptive measures against such a scenario, such mitigative actions in effect become a form of "tail risk" hedge to SWF portfolios.

4.3.2 Deficit Countries

The policy implications to deficit countries are as follows:

(1) *In good times and in bad* — Investee countries should recognize the need to create friendly investment environments in good times, so that politically it will be more palatable for foreign governments to join a rescue effort when things are not going well. Excessively protectionist policies help neither side. National security concerns should be addressed by two-way conversations instead of unilateral policies under ambiguous guidelines.

(2) *Rescues are not debtors' entitlements* — Deficit countries must get their public finances in order and avoid running clearly unsustainable levels of debt. Long gone are the days when unsuspecting central banks in developing countries would buy developed country public debts *en masse* in order to hold down the values of their own export currencies. Debtor countries are finding out the hard way that creditors (especially taxpayers of rescuer countries) can demand to know how the debtors propose to pay down new debts raised in distressed situations.

(3) *It's the economy, stupid* — There is nothing inherently wrong about raising new debts if the financing can result in economic growth to repay the debts. Many debtor countries do have the technological expertise that will lead to genuine innovation and productivity growth. The key is that debtor countries

must demonstrate that they can put sound policies in place, so that any public borrowing will stand a credible chance of translating into tangible investments and economic growth, not just consumption and unproductive public spending.

4.3.3   *New Gold Standard*

Finally, future research should focus on finding possible solutions to the problem of persistent global imbalance:

(1) *Balanced monetary policy* — Surplus countries used to be price takers. Debtor governments were able to set debt prices with almost one-sided monetary policy levers. Increasingly, investors like SWFs are big enough so that they are in the position to bargain. Unless debtor governments recognize this new reality, there will be endless squabbling over exchange and interest rates, while no debtor government can get on with the more serious business of fostering economic growth and productive investments.

(2) *Universal reserve asset* — One way or another, the world will probably end up adopting a universal reserve asset that is not controlled by any one single country. The real questions are when and how. Such an asset will be similar to the Special Drawing Rights (SDRs) created by the IMF[8], except that it must be universally accepted as a medium of exchange just like gold bullion — thus the idea of a "New Gold Standard" that does not impose an artificial constraint on the monetary base. Otherwise, thanks to the rapid proliferation in internet and mobile technologies, eventually a brilliant inventor will come up with a new electronic medium of exchange that addresses the known technical shortcomings of bitcoin. Central banks around the world need to show leadership or risk becoming increasingly marginalized.

(3) *Counter-cyclical policies* — Persistent imbalance has never ended well for all parties involved. The world needs a global financial economic system that is capable of self-correction. Unlike in the past, researchers now have access to massive computer clusters that can be used to construct far more complex system models to do realistic global simulations on plausible policy outcomes. Policy makers should no longer rely on parsimonious models driven by a handful of simultaneous equations, with the realistic possibility of not fully appreciating these models' unintended consequences.

---

[8]See http://www.imf.org/external/np/exr/facts/sdr.htm.

4.4 Summary

The global financial economy is at a crossroads. Policy makers have two simple choices. They can react to rapidly unfolding market events by putting on one band-aid at a time, thereby creating the potential need for more "push down, pop up" policy responses down the road, or they can think through plausible scenarios ahead of time to work out how best to respond. Although no one has a crystal ball, it is possible for SWFs to put together an investment framework that will help them navigate the new global financial landscape. In this chapter, we have provided some realistic examples of how a large state investor can work through its investment choices under some plausible market scenarios. None of the investment policy recommendations described in this chapter is dramatically new or groundbreaking. It is a matter of assembling the right analytical tools into a practical investment framework, so that a SWF can make effective investment decisions in real time. A close analogy is that a modern 100,000-ton aircraft carrier needs to be steered by differential thrust on propellers and bow thrusters, instead of simply relying on any "old school" analog rudder.

Chapter 5

Conclusions

This relatively concise book should have demystified some common misconceptions about sovereign wealth management for its audience:

(1) *Sovereign Wealth Funds are symbols of national strength* — Countries create sovereign wealth funds only when they are accumulating massive excess reserves in the form of claims on other countries. Usually, these claims significantly exceed what may be deemed necessary as foreign exchange reserves to maintain the stability of a country's currency. As these claims represent future promises by other countries to repay, they can be both a blessing and a curse. Although British authorities are proud of the fact that there has been no default on British government debts over the last three centuries, ultra long-term debts (such as those with maturity of 50 years) often face rapid depreciation on the values of their principals (in terms of purchasing power) when finally repaid. In 1923, France and Belgium occupied the Ruhr when Germany fell behind on war reparation payments, under the French belief that they had the right to extract the reparations themselves in the form of coal and steel. Historically, claims on real assets have always been seen as more superior than counting on paper promises.

(2) *It is always a sound investment policy to convert resource wealth into financial wealth as a means to diversify national balance sheets* — As discussed in the last point, real assets have certain obvious appeals over financial assets. However, if every central bank or SWF simultaneously invests in one or more commodities, the net effect will be equivalent to a form of mass hoarding, which is why most of them avoid doing so at least publicly. A more practical form of diversification is for resource-rich countries to enter into long-term barter agreements with one another. However, such interactions can get complicated when the price of real assets are set in terms of paper assets way

ahead of time, especially paper assets which supplies can be manipulated by official institutions around the world. The difficulty lies in setting a fair and sufficiently stable "exchange rate" between specific paper and real assets, in ways that do not cause artificial disruptions to resource production.

(3) *SWF can help countries diversify national balance sheets by selecting sound investments overseas* — There is no compelling evidence that SWF managers have any competitive advantages over their commercial counterparts in selecting alpha. In general, their massive size creates a hindrance for them to invest a meaningful sum in any investment, as long as such an investment is expected to create a material impact on performance. That often limits their investable universe to higher-market-capitalization investments, which are far more likely to produce performance similar to market indices because of the higher probability that such investments may already be large index components. As a result, typical SWF performance is mostly driven by asset allocation instead of alpha selection. In addition, there is no objective reason that countries can make a better return by finding investment opportunities outside their domestic economies, instead of pursuing traditional industrial policies by using national wealth to subsidize the early-stage growth of domestic industries, which has had some remarkable success among certain East Asian countries. On the contrary, making long-term investments outside of a country's home jurisdiction without direct policy levers has never been particularly promising, and countries can choose to make non-industrial investments for the purpose of extracting complementary agriculture or mineral resources from other countries.

(4) *SWF is essential to global financial stability as the "rescuer" of last resort* — The root cause of financial instability witnessed today is global imbalance. That does not imply that SWFs should be blamed for causing global imbalance, but their pervasive presence is in fact a direct consequence of persistent global imbalance. Instead of accumulating wealth in a SWF, a surplus country always has the simple option of putting its surplus wealth directly in the hands of its citizens. Once its citizens purchase goods and services from abroad or make direct overseas investments, the reverse outflow will allow the global imbalance of payments to self-correct. The existence of massive SWFs may also contribute indirectly to the prolonging of global imbalance; by rescuing institutions that should have been allowed to fail, SWFs could have inadvertently prolonged any economic malaise, until the point when even the

most aggressive central bank and SWF policy actions can no longer contain a snowballing financial crisis.

(5) *SWF is a more effective vehicle for investment professionals to invest national savings on behalf of a surplus country's citizens* — A surplus country may distribute its surplus wealth directly to its citizens as in a typical retirement plan, allowing its citizens to choose from several common investment profiles such as growth, balanced and conservative. Its citizens may also choose to deploy some of their entitlements for legitimate overseas investment purposes that can avoid the adverse economic effects of Dutch disease. For instance, one family may choose to buy a house in the US so that their children have a place to stay while attending American universities. Doing so fits well with their financial profiles and potentially maximizes their terminal wealth, by eliminating many "agency costs" involved in a less direct arrangement. It is unlikely that any professional investors can cater to these very specific invest-ment profiles, so there is no logical reason to believe that investment profes-sionals can do a better job in investing a family's entitlement than they can do so themselves. Moreover, professionals can help only up to a certain point, since they are limited by their frequent inability to deploy a huge sum of assets in aggregate, except in low-yielding Government bond markets.

The above is not meant to suggest that SWFs do not add value. This book is simply stating the obvious by pointing out that, like all other professional investors, no SWF has a magic wand. When a SWF is given the right analytical tools and adopts an effective investment framework, it can add value to its government clients. This book provides some examples of how SWFs can do so given their evolving role in today's global economy:

(1) *SWFs should adopt an institutional investment framework to clearly demon-strate that they are adding value to their end-investors* — It is difficult for typical SWFs to demonstrate significant out-performance relative to the mar-ket. Their size is often so massive that, at some point, they become the mar-ket. However, if all SWFs decide to go passive, that will be bad news too for the global economy, since innovation requires venture-style entrepreneur-ship typically not achievable by R&D spending made by bureaucratic large-capitalization companies alone. The practical solution is for SWFs to im-plement an institutional investment framework similar to those commonly used by the largest commercial asset management operations. Investment pro-fessionals at each level are incentivized to maximize active returns for their government clients. Likewise, more senior professionals should be asked to

"own" the allocation of capital between sub-asset classes. That way, SWFs can benefit from having a consistent investment framework to demystify the asset allocation process for their government clients and the people whom they are investing on behalf of.

(2) *SWFs should not be bashful about scenario and contingency planning* — In this book, we have provided some realistic examples of how a large state investor can work through its investment choices under some plausible market scenarios. Of course, putting together the analytical infrastructure to support portfolios of a typical SWF will be painstaking, but doing so is necessary for a SWF to make effective investment decisions in real time. A close analogy is that a modern 100,000-ton aircraft carrier cannot be steered by an "old school" analog rudder. Suffice it to say that there is no harm in conducting "planning drills" for all plausible scenarios and contingencies, since SWF portfolios cannot be turned "on a dime".

(3) *SWFs should accept their unique responsibilities as rescuers of last resort in today's global financial economy* — From a self-interest point of view, surplus economies may be ill-advised to force deficit economies into disorderly defaults, because the net exports terms on their national balance sheets may not recover after any such disorderly defaults, while there is no reason to believe that the values of their investments will necessarily hold up after disorderly defaults. Our analysis also shows that the most difficult risk for any SWF to hedge against is the risk of a potential global financial meltdown. Since SWFs are in the position to take preemptive measures against such a scenario, such mitigative actions in effect become a form of "tail risk" hedge to SWF portfolios.

Finally, how should the rest of the world adapt to the new reality of SWFs being significant and influential players in today's global economy?

(1) *Debtor countries need to put their public finances in order to avoid clearly unsustainable public debt levels* — Deficit countries must get their public finances in order and avoid running clearly unsustainable levels of debt. They are finding out the hard way that creditors (especially taxpayers of rescuer countries) can demand to know how the debtor proposes to pay down its new debts raised in a distressed situation. Many debtor countries do have the technological expertise that will lead to genuine innovation and productivity growth. The key is that debtor countries must demonstrate that they can put sound policies in place, so that any public borrowing will translate into

tangible investments and economic growth, not just pure consumption and/or unproductive public spending.

(2) *Policy makers should be prepared to agree on a more objective international reference currency* — One way or another, the world will probably end up adopting a universal reserve asset that is not controlled by any one single country. The real questions are when and how. Thanks to the rapid proliferation in internet and mobile technologies, eventually a brilliant inventor will come up with a new electronic medium of exchange that addresses the known technology shortcomings of bitcoin. Central banks around the world need to show leadership or risk becoming increasingly marginalized.

The world is now enjoying a time of plenty relative to most of human history. It is a good problem when researchers still have the luxury of time to work out how best to preserve large pockets of national wealth for multiple future generations. In terms of national priority, let's not forget that our discussions are meaningful only when human society is not facing basic survival challenges such as famine, disease, war and death. Those are the critical challenges that all human societies must first address, before spending time to think about accumulating, preserving and growing national economic wealth.

Bibliography

Ang, A., W. Goetzmann, and S. Schaefer, 2009, "A Broad Evaluation of Active Management of the Norwegian Government Pension Fund – Global," M2 Presswire.

Berk, J. and R. Green, 2004, "Mutual Fund Flows and Performance in Rational Markets," *Journal of Political Economy*, 112(6): 1269–1295.

Bernstein, S., J. Lerner, and A. Schoar, 2009, "The Investment Strategies of Sovereign Wealth Funds," Boston, USA: Harvard Business School Working Paper.

Chang, H.-J., 2010, *23 Things They Don't Tell You about Capitalism*, London, UK: Penguin.

Dyck, A. and A. Morse, 2010, "How and Why Do Sovereign Wealth Funds Tilt Their Portfolios," Chicago, USA: University of Chicago Working Paper.

Fung, W., D. Hsieh, N. Naik, and T. Ramadorai, 2008, "Hedge Funds: Performance, Risk, and Capital Formation," *Journal of Finance*, 63(4): 1777–1803.

Johan, S., A. Knill, and N. Mauck, 2011, "Determinants of Sovereign Wealth Fund Investment in Private Equity," Paper presented at the European Financial Management Symposium 2011.

Keating, C. and W. F. Shadwick, 2005, *Omega: Function and Metrics*, Cambridge, UK: Gilmour Drummond.

Lee, B., 2006, "Robust Portfolio Construction in a Sovereign Wealth Context," in J. Johnson-Calari and M. Rietveld (eds.), *Sovereign Wealth Management*, London, UK: Central Banking Publications.

Lee, B., 2009, "A Brief History of Hedge Fund Failures," Case Study, Singapore: BNP Paribas Hedge Fund Centre.

Lee, B., 2011a, "How Asia Can Best Use Its Surpluses," Op Ed, Singapore: *The Straits Times* (31 August).

Lee, B., 2011b, "The Unfolding of a Greek Tragedy," Op Ed, Singapore: *The Straits Times* (12 October).

Lee, B., 2011c, "More Global Imbalances Ahead," Op Ed, Singapore: *The Straits Times* (11 November).

Lee, B. and Y. Lee, 2004a, "The Alternative Sharpe Ratio," in B. Schachter (ed.), *Intelligent Hedge Fund Investing*, London, UK: Risk Books.

Lee, Y. and B. Lee, 2004b, "How 'Sharpe' are Funds of Funds?" in B. Schachter (ed.), *Intelligent Hedge Fund Investing*, London, UK: Risk Books.

Lee, B., D. Rogal, and F. Weinberger, 2010, "Strategic Asset Allocation and Portfolio Construction for Sovereign Wealth Managers," in A. Berkelaar, J. Coche, and K. Nyholm (eds.), *Central Bank Reserves and Sovereign Wealth Management*, New York, USA: Macmillan.

Lee, B. and H. Wang, 2011, "Reevaluating the Roles of Large Public Surpluses and Sovereign Wealth Funds in Asia," Tokyo, Japan: Asian Development Bank Institute Working Paper.

Merton, R. C., 1998, "Optimal Investment Strategies for University Endowment Funds," in W. Ziemba and J. Mulvey (eds.), *Worldwide Asset and Liability Modeling*, Cambridge, UK: Cambridge University Press.

Sachs, J., M. Kawai, J.-W. Lee, and W. T. Woo, 2010, *The Future Global Reserve System — An Asian Perspective*, New York, USA: ADB-Earth Institute Report (June).

Stiglitz, J. E., J. A. Ocampo, S. Spiegel, R. Ffrench-Davis, and D. Nayyar, 2006, *Stability with Growth: Macroeconomics, Liberalization and Development*, Oxford, UK: Oxford University Press.

Sun, T. and H. Hesse, 2009, "Sovereign Wealth Funds and Financial Stability — an Event Study Analysis," Washington DC, USA: IMF Working Paper.

Index